PUFFIN BOOKS

How to be a Teenage Millionaire

di James is an author, TV expert and business trainer who has
d her own body-language series on prime-time TV. As a teenager
di was much too distracted by boys and shopping to make any
ney but in *Teenage Millionaire* she has put together the type of
s that she wishes she'd read then!

James Moore is a journalist who has written for the *Daily Express*,
nday Telegraph and *Daily Mirror*. He also co-wrote the book *Blagging*
How to Get Almost Everything on the Cheap. James's first published
ce, for a national puzzle magazine, was a maze in the shape of an
g-timer. He was 10 years old and he was paid £5.

www.teenmillionaire.co.uk

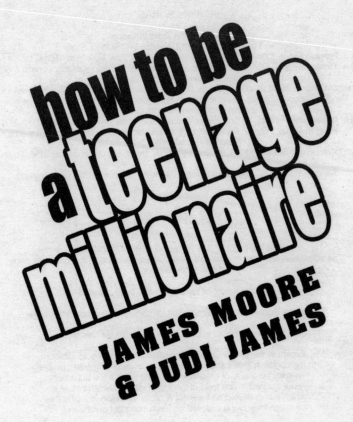

how to be a teenage millionaire

JAMES MOORE
& JUDI JAMES

PUFFIN

PUFFIN BOOKS

Published by the Penguin Group
Penguin Books Ltd, 80 Strand, London WC2R 0RL, England
Penguin Group (USA) Inc., 375 Hudson Street, New York, New York 10014, USA
Penguin Group (Canada), 90 Eglinton Avenue East, Suite 700, Toronto, Ontario, Canada M4P 2Y3
(a division of Pearson Penguin Canada Inc.)
Penguin Ireland, 25 St Stephen's Green, Dublin 2, Ireland (a division of Penguin Books Ltd)
Penguin Group (Australia), 250 Camberwell Road, Camberwell, Victoria 3124, Australia
(a division of Pearson Australia Group Pty Ltd)
Penguin Books India Pvt Ltd, 11 Community Centre, Panchsheel Park, New Delhi – 110 017, India
Penguin Group (NZ), 67 Apollo Drive, Rosedale, North Shore 0632, New Zealand
(a division of Pearson New Zealand Ltd)
Penguin Books (South Africa) (Pty) Ltd, 24 Sturdee Avenue, Rosebank, Johannesburg 2196, South Africa

Penguin Books Ltd, Registered Offices: 80 Strand, London WC2R 0RL, England

puffinbooks.com

First published 2007
1

Text copyright © Judi James and James Moore 2007
The acknowledgements on page 214 constitute an extension of this copyright page
All rights reserved

The moral right of the authors has been asserted

Typeset by Palimpsest Book Production Limited, Grangemouth, Stirlingshire

Made and printed in England by Clays Ltd, St Ives plc

British Library Cataloguing in Publication Data
A CIP catalogue record for this book is available from the British Library

ISBN: 978-0-141-32316-9

IMPORTANT NOTICE ON WEBSITES

We've done our very best to make sure that the online information listed in this book is as appropriate,
accurate and up-to-date as possible at the time of going to press. However, information on the
Internet is liable to change. Website addresses and website content are constantly being updated and
sites occasionally close down. In addition, there is the possibility that some websites may contain
material or links to material that may be unsuitable for children. Parents and guardians are strongly
advised to ensure that children's access to the Internet is supervised by a responsible adult.

The publishers cannot accept responsibility for any third party websites, or any material contained
in or linked to the same, or for any consequences arising from use of the Internet. Nor can we
guarantee that any website or URL shown in this book will be exactly as shown. If you wish to
comment on a website that is listed in this book, email us at *popular.culture@penguin.co.uk*

CONTENTS

FOREWORD

They say your first million is the hardest one to make. It takes talent, dedication and, above all, hard work before you can buy that sports car or retire to a desert island.

By reading this book you are thinking about where your talents lie and how you might fulfil your ambitions. But you don't have to be top of the class or from a rich family to succeed.

As a charity The Prince's Trust helps thousands of young people every year who are less fortunate than most. They might have a dream, but not the support from family and friends that is vital when starting out. We help these young people by giving them the confidence to believe in themselves and the motivation to turn their dreams into reality. It's truly amazing what a relatively small amount of support can achieve.

Two young men from Huddersfield came to The Prince's Trust with a basic business plan. Neither James nor Simon had done very well at school, but they did have a talent for art and a passion to do something they enjoyed. Their dream was to start a design company and work for some of the biggest brands in the world.

The Prince's Trust provided them with a grant and practical advice so they could set up their first office in James's grandmother's attic, which was the inspiration for their company name 'Attik'. After 18 years, their company has offices in New York, San Francisco and, of course, Huddersfield, and makes £10 million a year.

The key is to have a positive attitude – to believe in yourself and your abilities. And remember, when Bill Gates was creating the world's largest company and became the world's richest man, he also became the biggest charitable giver in history.

Martina Milburn
Chief Executive
The Prince's Trust

START MILLI-THINKING NOW!

Have you ever wondered how it would feel to be the next big business supremo, like easyJet's Stelios or TV entrepreneur Peter Jones? Maybe you fancy yourself as a premier football star, like Ryan Giggs? Or perhaps playing for England, like cricketer Isa Guha? Do you long to be a singing sensation, like Katie Melua or even Katherine Jenkins? Or maybe you see yourself up there on the big screen, like *Harry Potter*'s Rupert Grint?

This book is chock-full of interviews with top people in every walk of life who are prepared to share their tips and advice on how you can make success happen. Not all of these star names are millionaires. Some are indeed megarich, but what they all have in common is the kind of 'milli-thinking' that's taken them to the top – the desire to do something to the best of their abilities and use their talents to make things happen. They all began their adventure while young, so who better to ask how to be successful than the people who have been there and done it?

You don't have to be brainy, beautiful or bold as brass to be a milli-thinker like them. Even age isn't a barrier – some of our most successful names were busy being successful while they were still at school. This book is going to tell you how to develop what you have already got and get milli-thinking for yourself. It's about finding your talent and making the most of it, whether it makes you rich or not.

As well as hearing from the stars you'll find step-by-step suggestions to help you achieve success in business, sport, music, drama and through the Internet, along with practical advice. You'll be given organizations and websites that can help you take your ambitions further and, with fun facts and great brain boxes to help get that grey matter into gear, you'll be thinking and achieving success in no time.

Waiting till you're old to follow your dreams is so last century. Whatever your ambition, this book can help make it happen. Even if you're stuck for inspiration, it will show you how to identify exactly what your dream might be.

How to be a Teenage Millionaire is the ultimate guide to kick-starting your brilliant life.

1.
BECOME AN APPRENTICE MILLIONAIRE

Why It Could Be You

Right now the millionaire dream might seem a long way from your comfortable couch. But if you're keen to join the ranks of the brightest and the best then it's time to get started. Because, whoever you are, reaching the top is within your grasp!

The people who achieve big success in life – and especially those who make it big while still young – aren't always the ones who shone at school or shouted the loudest. What made the difference was the desire to decide their own future, the ability to set their own goals, do something creative or try something that had never been done before.

MILLI-FACT
There are over 150 people in Britain with the surname Million.

This chapter is about how to start milli-thinking, so you can focus on your fab future. First you'll be thinking about who you are and what you want out of life. Then you'll read about some of the brilliantly successful individuals out there who have made it happen. You may be surprised by what a real mixed bunch they are – just like you and your mates.

Some milli-myths (those fears about how difficult it is to find success) are going to be blasted out of the water before you find out about the qualities you need to make your own dream into a reality.

Give yourself one big tick straight away, because you already have something very useful indeed – your age. Check out why with our first brain box, one of loads in the book aimed at firing up your mental powers.

BRAIN BOX
Why Being Young Is Useful

See if you agree with some of the following statements about yourself. You probably do. That's what makes you the perfect wannabe.

★ I really believe that anything is possible for my own future.
★ I love my friends and family but in the end I know that the future is in my hands alone.
★ I always want to ask questions.
★ I'm stubborn and don't like shelling out for stuff.
★ I feel excited about the idea of winning and success.
★ I'm good at cutting through the waffle others talk – I get to the point.
★ I get passionate about things and don't see negatives all the time.
★ I have the right to do well.
★ I have bags of energy and enthusiasm.
★ I know what people like me want.

So how do you start building your own success story? First, you've got to think about your own values: where are you coming from, what do you want to achieve . . . and how?

Working Out Your Milli-Values

Think about yourself. What have you done that has felt like a success? Don't just think things like exam passes, think of things that you really feel proud of, even if they didn't win you an award or a mention in the local newspaper. Make a list.

Seeing Your Own Success

Success isn't always easy to spot in yourself. But it's vital to know what you're good at and what all your strengths are if you're going to point your life in the right direction. Sometimes it's easier to list all the things you can't do, but why sit there focusing on the negative when you could be developing all your positive skills? When you've finished your success list, make another list of all the things you intend to succeed at or do well in. Goals give you something to work on. How high should those targets be? Try it. Test it out. Push it further than you think. You could be amazed at the result!

Years ago no one had run a mile in under four minutes and most people thought it was impossible. Then in 1954 Roger Bannister did it. What happened next? Lots of people started to break the four-minute barrier. Everyone moved on to the next target. It just shows that you never know what's possible until you try.

Success comes in all sorts of shapes and sizes too. You've probably forgotten a whole load of your achievements to date, but there are things you're doing every day that you should be calling achievements even if they don't seem that huge. Here are some thoughts to get you going.

Caring success:

★ Do you help or care for people or pets?

★ Do you mentor other kids at school?

★ Do you help people when you're out?

★ Do you cheer people up or make them laugh?

★ Do you work for a charity?

★ Are you a good listener?

Personal success:

★ Do you exercise regularly?

★ Have your learnt any new skills or started any hobbies, like playing an instrument or taking photos?

★ Do you care about your appearance?

★ Do you look friendly and sociable?

Personal challenges:

★ Have you ever pushed yourself physically?

★ Have you ever achieved beyond your normal levels of self-confidence, like speaking up in class or doing well in an interview?

★ Have you overcome any phobias?

★ Have you ever been brave, even if it's something like going to the doctor for an injection?

★ Have you had any illness or injury and overcome it?

Personal values:

★ Do you have an interest in issues like the environment or helping others?

★ Do you care about your health and eating well?

★ Do you care about the treatment of other people?

★ Do you try to behave well to others?

★ Are you concerned about issues like racism, sexism or bullying?

Team values:

★ How many 'teams' do you belong to? This includes groups like your family, school class and friends.

★ How good are you at working as a member of those teams?

★ Are you able to put others first?

★ Are you good at looking at joint goals, rather than just personal ones?

★ Are you able to change your role in the team, acting as leader when it's needed but backing down when appropriate?

★ Do you trust other people and win their trust too?

★ Are you a good sport?

It's important to give yourself credit for everything you achieve. The world is full of successful people who don't have their names in the newspaper or faces on TV. Success can take many different forms – the key is finding the right fit for you.

Value-Added Acts

As well as thinking 'What do I want to do?', ask yourself: 'Who do I want to be?' There are loads of top business people who ask themselves not only 'What did I do today?' at the end of every day but also '*How* did I do it?' This way they can check they're on track with their own set of values. Focusing on you and the way you work and conduct yourself is every bit as important as focusing on what you're doing.

Write Out Your Own 'Life Code'

How do you want to behave? What do you feel is a good way to live with other people? List personal values in relation to yourself. Jobs and careers are important if you plan to be successful, but so is the way you choose to work. After all, you're a human *being* not a human *doing*.

Here's a fun scenario that links your personal values to success. You notice it's been a very cold winter and everyone at school is shivering because the heating has broken down. You decide some furry ear-wigs would be just the thing to warm up your mates. They cost very little to make and you run up a couple of dozen over the weekend to take into school. Do you:

(a) Give them away as presents?
(b) Sell them for what it cost to make them?
(c) Sell them at the cost price plus a bit more for the time you spent making them?
(d) Sell them for a big profit because you know your mates are desperate?

There's no right answer, apart from what your personal set of values tells you is right.

How Would You Like Other People to Describe You?

It might sound grim but write your own obituary (what's written about you after you're dead). People in business or the arts who are 'value-aware' often do this to make sure they can be proud of the way they're living.

Find Charities That Interest You

Everyone has causes that are important to them. By finding yours, you'll not only get to meet like-minded people but also have a taste of what it's like to organize, come up with ideas, communicate and take action, as well as working in a group that's new to you.

Take On a Local Cause

Try to raise funds for a new play park or for repairing the local youth club. Try the Internet to see what's in your area.

MILLI-FACT

There are now more than 425,000 millionaires in the UK. That's about 1 in every 142 people.

OK, so you're thinking about your abilities and values, but there might still seem a big gap between you and those high-achieving heroes of yours.

In fact they all had to start somewhere. Let's burst a few milli-myths – the reasons why you think you can't do something and all the reasons why you can. The odds of winning big on the Lottery are 14,000,000 to 1. Your odds of being a top businessman, actor or sports star are much better than that.

And remember, there are a million ways to make it!

Milli-Myth 1: You Have to be Top of the Class

Wrong! Think: James Morrison. Doing well at school is always going to help you get a better career, but not doing as well as you'd hoped in tests and exams doesn't mean you should shelve your ambitions or dreams.

Take James Morrison, the Brit award winner who is at the top of the music game and selling bucketloads of records in his early twenties. Amazingly the star actually failed his A level in music. He got a U for Ungraded. Though he struggled with the academic side of studying music, he still enjoyed getting out there and playing his guitar. He started his career in pop by busking, sometimes making up to £70 an hour.

Top psychologist Richard Wiseman reckons you don't have to be the brainiest person to have a great idea. You just have to spot something – whether it's an invention or a great tune – that other people haven't hit on yet. That takes thought, but not necessarily a telephone-number-sized IQ. Work on your hobbies and join clubs to see how you can use your talents, even if they don't seem to shine in the classroom. A bad mark or grade may feel like the end of the world, but it never is.

BANK ON THIS

Five Millionaires Who Shone Despite Dodgy Exam Results

John Terry: He knew that footie skills were his ticket to success. At 16 he joined a YTS scheme at Chelsea FC. At first he was earning only £46 a week. But it was worth it. He went on to captain England.

Philip Green: The billionaire boss of stores like Topshop and Burton was itching to get into business from an early age. He left school at 15, but his lack of qualifications didn't mean he slouched around. Phillip went to work as a shoe importer before starting to sell women's clothes. Today he is worth a staggering £3.76 billion.

Lily Allen: She's a chart-topping solo artist. But Lily didn't do well at school and admits that her only qualification is in flower arranging! Musical success didn't just land in her lap though: she started her own MySpace site and got her tunes out there.

Guy Ritchie: When Guy parted company with his school in Hertfordshire at 15 he quickly got a job that tallied with his passion for movies – as a runner on film sets. Later he made the smash-hit gangster movie *Lock, Stock and Two Smoking Barrels*. He also married Madonna.

Robbie Williams: A pop sensation who, rather than 'giving up' when he failed his GCSEs, got involved in theatre groups and motivated himself to go to an audition for a new boy band. It turned out to be Take That . . .

Milli-Myth 2: You Have to be Loud and Brash

Wrong! Think: Bill Gates. He's the richest man in the world. But he was a shy, lonely kid. Everyone thought he would become a lawyer like his dad, but Bill had other plans. Sure, he was quiet, but he still had confidence in his own abilities. He went on to set up Microsoft and became the youngest-ever self-made billionaire at the age of 31.

It might amaze you to know that in a survey of top company bosses only six out of ten had outgoing personalities. In fact, being shy isn't a barrier to success, whether you're aiming to be a business whizz or to go on the stage.

BANK ON THIS
Four Shy Millionaires

Steven Spielberg: The director of *Jaws* and *Jurassic Park* was a shy kid who had a complex about his nose. By the age of 12 he had already funded his own film from a tree-planting business and by charging admission to see his own home-made movies.

Richard Branson: The Virgin boss has dabbled in everything from planes to phones and is now a household name worth £3 billion. Yet he says he has always been shy and has had to force himself to make speeches.

David and Frederick Barclay: These two newspaper and retail tycoons are worth £1.5 billion. You'd think they would want to shout about it, but they bought an uninhabited island in the Channel Islands to live like hermits.

John Caudwell: He is a mobile-phone millionaire who made £1.46 billion from the sale of his Phones4U business. He didn't let being bullied at school stop him from showing off his muscles in business.

Milli-Myth 3: Your Talent Has to be Obvious

Wrong! Think: Simon Cowell. *X Factor* judge Simon Cowell wouldn't have got far as a singer. But, of course, he does have a talent – a knack of spotting a future star and then helping them to zoom up the charts. Like Simon, who started his career in the post room of a record company, your talent might not seem obvious at first. But it's there. You have something to offer. Everyone does. The point is to identify it and use it – even if it's something unusual. Try out different things and take time to focus on your 'little something' so that you can build it into something big.

BANK ON THIS
Two Unusual Ways to a Million

Trevor Baylis: Who would have thought a clockwork radio could make you a million? It did for Trevor. His simple wind-up radio proved a huge hit in Africa, where few people can afford electricity or batteries.

Ted Prosser: He did it by accident. While decorating he fell off his ladder and nudged a bottle of thinned filler over the coat of paint he had just applied. It helped him create Ronseal's Paint and Grain, which three years later was worth £10 million in sales.

Milli-Myth 4: You Have to be One of the Gang

Wrong! Think: Warren Buffet. The US businessman is worth £25 billion. He bought his first shares when he was 11. He describes himself as an introvert, and reckons that helped him stand out from the crowd when dealing on the stock market.

At school, being an outsider doesn't always seem to help much. But in the real world, being different means that you might come up with something no one has thought of yet. Or maybe you'll just have the nerve to back yourself instead of following the herd.

BANK ON THIS

Three Eccentric Millionaires

Scott Alexander: This wacky young British millionaire is pretty pleased with himself. Worth £3 million by the time he was 31, he made his money advising super-rich people on how to get the ultimate body. Then he bought an entire Bulgarian seaside resort and named it after himself. He said, 'I've decided to call it Alexander, which I suppose is quite cheeky.' He also devoted one wall of his Manchester home to a £10,000 portrait of himself!

Percy Shaw: He was a road repairer who invented the cat's eye – those little reflective things in the middle of the road. He got the idea when the reflection from a real cat's eyes helped stop him swerving off the road at night. Though he made a million, he never had carpets put in his house, wore moth-eaten jumpers and used to watch several TVs at once.

J. Paul Getty, senior: This multi-millionaire oil magnate was so mean he installed payphones for guests to use in his home. When his grandson was kidnapped, he didn't pay a ransom until the kidnappers had sent the boy's severed ear to him to prove they actually had the child.

Milli-Myth 5: You Have to be Old

Wrong! Think: Sir Alan Sugar. The beardy boss from *The Apprentice* looks like he's been saying 'You're fired!' for centuries. But, believe it or not, he was once young too. The son of a tailor, he started flogging ginger beer at 11. By the time he left school at 16 he was earning more than his dad. Then he started selling car aerials out of the back of a van. Now he is worth £800 million, as well as being a TV star.

MILLI-FACT

According to official figures, there were 432 company directors in the UK aged less than 16 in 2006, of which just fewer than half were under 10.

BANK ON THIS

Four Millionaires Who Started Young

Shirley Temple: The youngest-ever self-made millionaire was this American, who banked $1 million before she was 10.

Dominic McVey: He was 13 when he started the craze for collapsible mini-scooters and made a million by the time he was 15.

Sir Clive Sinclair: He's famous for designing a one-person vehicle called the C5 that was, frankly, a bit of a flop. Much more successful were his designs for pocket calculators and the ZX81 computer. He started by earning money from mowing lawns and washing up. Then he took holiday jobs at electronics companies. By the time he was 18 he knew that he could make money selling miniature electronic kits for enthusiasts by mail order.

Richard Desmond: A media tycoon who got a job as a cloakroom attendant at a publishing group aged 14. By 21 he had his own house. Now he owns the *Daily Express* and is worth £700 million.

Milli-Myth 6: You Have to Like Wearing Suits

The idea of wearing a suit and sitting in a stuffy office all day makes some people run for the hills. But you don't have to sit behind a desk to make a million. Think of all those successful people who have used natural abilities like singing, acting or playing sport. You have to become good enough and – just as important – make sure you don't blow it all with a silly lifestyle once you get a whiff of fame.

BANK ON THIS

Four Millionaires Who Used Their Natural Abilities

Michelle Wie: Who says a girl can't enter the millionaire club by playing golf. She did, by turning pro at 15 and teeing up a $10 million fortune.

Daniel Radcliffe: The *Harry Potter* star didn't get to be a millionaire by magic. He got it through using his talent for acting and hard work.

Joss Stone: She found fame as a teenage singer and, according to *The Sunday Times* Rich List, is now worth around £5 million.

Jamie Oliver: The TV chef who turned us on to his cooking found the ingredients for financial success too and helped loads of others achieve their kitchen career dreams along the way.

Milli-Myth 7: You Have to be Obsessed with Making Money

Wrong! Think: Tim Berners-Lee. Not exactly a household name, Tim invented the World Wide Web, the system that allows us to see all the stuff on the Internet. He wasn't driven by making millions, he just loved tinkering with technology. At an early age he was pretending to make computers out of cardboard boxes. Later, at university, he built a basic one by modifying a TV set.

After creating the World Wide Web you'd have thought he'd go on to set up a huge profit-making company. Instead Tim preferred an academic life to riches and the limelight, and he went off to enjoy a much more modestly paid university career.

So success doesn't mean greed. Lots of tycoons and celebrities go on to use their skills to set up charities.

BANK ON THIS
Tycoons and Stars Giving It Back

Bill Gates: He has stumped up $28 billion to help tackle health issues around the globe, including the fight against AIDS.

David Beckham: The multi-millionaire footballer is helping grass-roots football with the David Beckham Academy: *www.thedavidbeckhamacademy.com*

Bono: The U2 singer is just as famous for his charity work and teaming up with Bob Geldof on Live Aid as for his music.

Andrew Reynolds: Founder of the Entrepreneur Channel, he recently gave away £100,000 in loans of £10 to teens who wanted to start a business.

Anita Roddick: Body Shop founder, she has promised to give away her millions, saying, 'I don't want to die rich.'

Sandra Bullock: A generous actress who has donated $1 million for earthquake relief efforts in Asia and Africa, as well as another $1 million to the American Red Cross in the wake of 9/11.

Tools for the Top

From business to football there are some qualities that the biggest and the best tend to share. Here's some milli-thinking musts to help inspire you.

Milli-Must 1: Think Big

Right! Think: Peter Jones (from TV's *Dragons' Den*). The pinstriped tycoon describes himself as a 'serial entrepreneur'. When young, he had the kind of vision that's typical of a budding millionaire-in-the-making. He says, 'I always wanted to do the best I could. I knew that one day I was going to be a multi-millionaire.' Most millionaires aim for the highest goals. Once they achieve them, they think up some more goals to aim for.

MILLI-FACT

The richest man in history was John Rockefeller, an oil man whose wealth topped £100 billion.

Milli-Must 2: Be Idea Alert

Right! Think: Steve Jobs (man behind the iPod). Always be on the lookout for good ideas. Often these can be just common-sense solutions to everyday problems. The key is to know that people will want it. Asked why Apple developed the iPod, chief executive Steve Jobs replied that he thought existing digital players didn't look cool enough. His genius wasn't only to come up with a revolutionary product, it was to give it a design that people would want to be seen using.

BANK ON THIS

Three Millionaires in the Making?

Jake Lunn: He was 8 when he got his big vision. While on holiday he was leafing through a sailing magazine when a flashy boat caught his eye. He promptly declared he was going to buy it. It was there that his business idea for making personalised printed napkins for yachts was born. Now 10, he claims to have 'about £1,000 in my bank account'.

Luisa Bundy: She turned her kitchen-table hobby for making toys into a business. By the time she was 15 her Little Bundies figures were selling in the top London toy store, Hamleys.

Fraser Doherty: At 17 this food fanatic was already MD of his own company, making jam from his grandma's old recipe and turning over £5,000 a month.

Milli-Must 3: Value Yourself

Right! Think: Sahar Hashemi (co-founder of Coffee Republic who sold her share for £15 million). Sahar and her brother were turned down by 19 banks before they got funding for what later proved to be a brilliant business idea.

They believed in themselves – and so must you. It doesn't matter if you're nervous, shy or a worrier as long as you've got drive and enthusiasm. You might even be stubborn. That will work too, especially when the chips are down and things aren't quite going your way. Often it's not how you act normally that makes you successful, it's how you act under pressure.

MILLI-FACT

If you could pile up one million £1 coins you'd have a tower standing 3.15 km high. That's around ten times the height of the Eiffel Tower in Paris.

Milli-Must 4: Keep the Faith

Right! Think: James Dyson (vacuum-cleaner king). Sometimes people won't see it your way, that your idea is as brilliant as you know it is. Listen to criticism and advice and then make a decision. If you still believe in your idea, go for it. That's exactly what James Dyson, one of Britain's richest men, did. He was the brains behind the bagless vacuum cleaner. When he was touting the idea around to get finance, no one wanted to know. He had more faith in himself. Using £10,000, he went ahead and built it anyway. Today he's cleaned up.

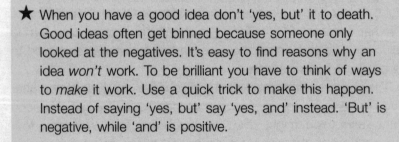

BRAIN BOX
Eight Ways to 'Think' Millionaire

★ When you have a good idea don't 'yes, but' it to death. Good ideas often get binned because someone only looked at the negatives. It's easy to find reasons why an idea *won't* work. To be brilliant you have to think of ways to *make* it work. Use a quick trick to make this happen. Instead of saying 'yes, but' say 'yes, and' instead. 'But' is negative, while 'and' is positive.

★ Listen to experience but make your own decisions. Just because an idea didn't work in the past doesn't mean it won't fly when the time is right.

★ Never, ever moan. It's wasted energy! It's easy to do, but working on your idea is far, far better. Take a look at people around you who moan. Do they ever achieve anything? Spend one day doing a moan audit. How many times do you moan? If it's a lot, stop.

★ Milli-thinking happens best when you're relaxed, which is when the inspirational, creative thoughts emerge. Keep a notebook by the side of your bed, bath or even the toilet to make sure those Eureka moments don't go unlogged.

★ See what your dreams and goals look like. Cut out a picture of the hero you're hoping to match and stick it in front of you while you work.

★ Write all your goals down. Studies at Harvard University in America proved students who did were much more successful in life than those who didn't.

★ Take exercise. It helps release positive and optimistic thoughts and moods. Sitting around can make your depressed.

★ Be your own cheerleader! Tell yourself how good you are now and again and praise yourself when you do well. It's better to be self-motivational than to look for reassurance and ego-boosting from other people. Remind yourself how great you are on a regular basis, only don't do it out loud or people might start giving you strange looks.

Milli-Must 5: Don't Worship Money – Know Its Worth

Right! Think: Lewis Bankes-Hughes (14-year-old with a bedroom business). You already know £1 million won't just magic itself into your bank account. If it's to get there at all you've got to start thinking about money and value it properly.

And you can even benefit from being young. Lewis Bankes-Hughes set up his graphic-design company, Fluffy Duster, doing graphic design from his own bedroom. He saved money because he was able to live at home and that enabled him to offer small businesses cheap rates to do graphics and websites.

There's nothing wrong with getting a part-time job either. Use it to pick up on how a particular business runs or to earn money to make your own project come true. You need to think about saving, earning and investing in your future.

BANK ON THIS
Use your Youth-Abilities

Negotiate: Practise your negotiating skills when you do the chores at home by, for example, negotiating a fee for taking on extra tasks.

Cash in on interests: Your ability to do things some adults don't understand can earn money. For example, charge teachers, relatives and friends' parents for setting up their computers, sorting out their phones or walking their pets. Identify activities that will save them money and time, and add to your savings.

Save money: Go and get your hair cut for free at a hairdressing school. Benefit from technology you understand by getting cheap or even free phone calls with new Internet services.

> **Cash in on youth culture:** One 18-year-old made a fortune by reading his younger sister's magazines to find out what was hot in teen culture and then buying up matching domain names on the web to make money from advertising. Think creatively and positively and look for potential in your everyday life.

Milli-Thinking Workouts

Confidence Boosting

Self-worth and self-confidence come in many shapes and sizes and to boost your self-esteem it's good to take a long hard look at your strengths and weaknesses.

Try defining your personality by describing yourself honestly on paper. Start by writing 'I am' then list all the words and roles that describe you. You can use physical descriptions like 'tall' or 'brown-haired', personality descriptions like 'shy' or 'talkative' and role descriptions like 'a sister' or 'cat-owner'. Now try turning those descriptions into positives. For instance, you could replace 'shy' with 'I like to be quiet with people until I know and understand them. I am good at sizing people up and understanding how they feel'. Or 'frizzy-haired' could become: 'I'm lucky to have thick hair that is naturally curly and full of energy.'

If you stick on any negatives like 'I'm lazy', start to do what's called 'creating future history'. This is working in a way to change yourself by redefining yourself. This means replacing 'I'm lazy', which is a statement of fact and unlikely to improve or change, with 'I used to sleep late or avoid jobs I don't like but now I attack everything with energy and avoid putting things off.' By altering your words you can alter your own view of yourself. This makes real change far more likely.

A key way to boost your self-confidence is to start talking about yourself in positive ways. It's too easy to talk yourself down without realizing it, sometimes in a bid to be funny or to get your friends to boost you up. It's also natural to think you're boasting if you don't do this. See how good you are at talking yourself down:

★ You're wearing a favourite top and someone says they like it. What's your reply? 'Oh, this is old, I just got it in a sale' or 'Thanks.'

★ Someone says how nice your hair looks. Do you think: 'They're taking the mickey, I know it needs cutting' or 'What they're really saying is they think it looked rubbish before' or 'That's nice'?

★ You get good grades in a test at school. Do you think: 'Brilliant, I've cracked it. The hard work paid off' or 'How on earth can I keep that up?'?

Don't stick to negative thoughts that make you less and less confident. Look at the positive ones. It might be difficult at first, but you only need to spend a short time policing your thoughts. Business people do it frequently, even the top ones. A thought like 'My nose is too big, I wish it was smaller' can be replaced with 'I like my nose, it makes me stand out.' Easy!

MILLI-MOUTH

‘Self-confidence is the first requisite to great undertakings.’ – *Samuel Johnson, writer*

Skill-Spotting for Beginners

It's important to know your own potential. The easiest way to do this is to talent-spot, picking out the things you're naturally good at or enjoy doing and seeing what they mean in terms of intelligence-mapping – finding out what type of success will suit you the best.

To get your thinking kick-started, try this quiz. Answer 'yes' or 'maybe' to each comment.

A

1. I'm very good at explaining things.
2. I enjoy talking and chatting.
3. I have a good imagination and think creatively.
4. I love writing stories and poems.
5. I'm good at telling jokes or stories.
6. I'm always sending texts or emails and I have my own blog.

B

1. I enjoy working on my computer.
2. I'm very good at planning and seeing things through.
3. I like to know how things work.
4. I'm very thorough and pay attention to details.
5. I prefer facts to fiction.
6. When I get upset I go quiet, rather than rant and rave.

C

1. I'm good at sports and love exercise.
2. I prefer the outdoors to indoors.
3. I admire people who push themselves.
4. I'm a good dancer.
5. I like to get on with things rather than wait around.
6. I enjoy action movies.

D

1. I'm a very good listener.
2. I'm good at imagining how other people feel.
3. I remember birthdays.

4. People come to me with their problems.
5. I get on with a wide range of people.
6. I hate to hurt or upset people.

Give yourself two points for every 'yes' answer and one for a 'maybe'. Add up all the points in each category and see what your key strengths are in terms of types of intelligence.

★ If you got your highest score for A, you're a natural performer or entertainer, with very good communication skills.

★ If you scored high for B, you're a logical thinker who enjoys technical jobs and tasks.

★ If C was your highest score, you're a born athlete or physical worker who likes making things or doing active work.

★ If D came out top, you're a people person, good at bonding with and understanding others. Rapport-building is high on your list of qualities.

MILLI-FACT

Only 2 per cent of those with the 'millionaire mind' scored high in school grades or IQ tests, according to researcher Stanley Thomas.

What Sort of Intelligence Have You Got?

Once you've looked at your skills you can start to understand your intelligence and strengths. Forget school IQ tests and exams, top boffins have discovered at long last that there's more than one way to be brainy. There are eight key intelligences, according to research at Harvard University, and any one of them can be enough to qualify you for the role of teen extraordinaire.

BRAIN BOX

Tap Into Your Intelligence Type

★ Linguistic: Are you a good speaker or writer? Are you good at explaining things?

★ Mathematical or logical: Are you good with figures? Can you focus on details and be thorough about logical things?

★ Visual or spatial: Do you have a good sense of direction? Are you observant, maybe noticing things others have missed? Do you use diagrams and maps easily?

★ Musical: Can you sing or play an instrument? Can you write songs?

★ People skills: Are you good at conversations and meeting new people? Do you tend to be popular and outgoing? Can you persuade and sell easily?

★ Bodily or physical: Are you good at sports or more physical activities? Are you skilful with your hands?

★ Naturalist: Are you into environmental issues or the weather? Do you have an affinity with nature?

★ Understanding: Can you always see the other person's point of view? Are you sensitive at reading other people's moods and feelings?

Any or all of these intelligences can be used to help fulfil your goals.

Here are some tips from one of telly's top motivational experts, Yolande Beckles of TV's *Don't Mess With Miss Beckles*, to give you a boost.

YOLANDE'S TOP TIPS

★ Motivation is vital. It doesn't matter who you are, you need to look at your own life differently. Who are you? Challenge things in your life. The main thing an entrepreneur needs is self-belief. You need to know you can succeed. That should be your starting point.

★ Sit down with a blank sheet of paper. Ask yourself 'Who am I?' Write down things you know about yourself. For instance, can you sing? Dance? Write down songs and music if that's your thing. Look at your list, then cross off any things you don't enjoy. Only leave the things you feel passionate about.

★ Act on the things you like. Go to local classes, get into training schools. See other people perform – at the theatre, ballet or opera – and be inspired by and learn from them.

★ Test yourself in the market. Go to workshops, use the Internet or magazines. Use your school as well – see what's available. Make friends with the teachers you like and who like you.

★ Keep a diary. Keep track of your dreams and keep links to your ideas and beliefs. Keep a record of what you're doing and how you're thinking.

★ Avoid giving up. Lots of people give up too early. If you don't get picked for the school football team, don't allow that to stop you playing football.

★ Take risks. Gamble and create things. Instead of getting money from your parents, work out how to buy things for yourself.

★ Start to discover your own strengths, even if they sound like negatives. Experiment with your skills.

All your heroes started off in life much like you. They were all born with traits or disadvantages that could have held them back. But what they all had in common was determination: they believed they could do it. By now you should be feeling that you're not so different from them after all, and that you can do it too.

Achieving your goals won't always be easy. But follow the advice and pointers in the following chapters and you'll soon have your foot on that ladder of success. Each chapter takes a look at a different area in which to try and make your mark.

As you read on, remember these five milli-thinking top tips:

★ What seems impossible now could be very possible.
★ Whoever you look up to is a human. They had setbacks and worries too.
★ Doing something is always better than doing nothing.
★ Keep dreaming, even if your dream changes with experience.
★ *You* are the most important person in building yourself a bright future.

2.
THINK LIKE AN ENTREPREN-AIRE

Becoming a successful entrepreneur starts with having ideas. But if the thought of coming up with the next big brainwave puts you off, don't worry: it's often the smallest and simplest ideas that show the best results. An entrepreneur is someone who sees something they want to change or improve – and then does it.

Some entrepreneurs build new industries from scratch or build companies that provide a first-rate service. Others use their entrepreneurial skills to improve society – whether it's starting a bank to lend money to the poor, like Muhammad Yunus, the Nobel peace prize winner and founder of the Grameen Bank in Bangladesh, or organizing a new local bus service to a deprived part of town, like Chrissie Townsend in East London.

MILLI-MOUTH

❝Obviously everyone wants to be successful, but I want to be looked back on as being very innovative, very trusted and ethical and ultimately making a big difference in the world.**❞** – *Sergey Brin, the guy behind search engine Google*

Follow the tips in this chapter and you could be bursting with schemes in no time, turning into the sort of person who gets stuck into your master plan rather than just sitting around thinking about it. You'll discover the qualities that are going to mark you out as a milli-thinking entrepreneur and find ways of improving those qualities to make the most of your creative ideas. You're going to find out how to spot brilliant opportunities and have the energy to make the most of them.

BANK ON THIS

Entrepreneurs in History: These Big-Thinking Types Have Always Been Around

Henry Ford: He realized that ordinary people wanted cars as well as posh folk. America's mass-produced Model T Ford revolutionized travel.

Walt Disney: He saw how people's passion for films and cartoons could be turned into a multi-million pound business that included theme parks.

Florence Nightingale: She helped nurse injured soldiers in the Crimean War. When she came home she set up a string of schools for nurses.

Anita Roddick: She could see that people wanted greener products and set up the Body Shop in the 1970s, a business that L'Oréal bought in 2006 for £650 million.

Ray Kroc: He saw the potential for fast food in the 1950s. He took McDonald's from one restaurant in the desert into a worldwide brand.

Bob Geldof: This musician turned his talents for entrepreneurship to organizing massive and unique concerts like Live Aid and Live 8, raising awareness and money to fight famine in Africa and encourage fair trade schemes for poor countries.

> **King Croesus:** He saw that minting coins could, er, make him a mint. Without the wily sixth-century BC monarch, entrepreneurs would probably still be doing deals by swapping goats.

In a world where everything changes as quickly as what's at number one, fresh thinking and enthusiasm are as prized as age and experience. It's to young guns like you that people are looking for new ideas!

There are three key steps to getting into the entrepreneur mindset:

Step 1: Find out about entrepreneur DNA.

Step 2: Understand how your money works.

Step 1: Be inspired.

Entrepreneur DNA – Have You Got It? How Can You Get It?

Many experts reckon there's a kind of entrepreneur DNA – qualities in some people that drive them to set up something new.

To test your current levels of entrepreneur DNA, start with this checklist of the 14 fab key qualities you'll need to crack the world of business. Spot all your key strengths first, and then look for any weak spots.

Your Entrepreneur Checklist

1. Goal power: Do you work to goals? Before you start a job do you imagine what the end result will look like? Knowing what you want is more valuable than knowing what you don't. Most young entrepreneurs started out with very firm goals in mind. What are yours?

2. Success specs: This is the ability to have vision – to think big and think ahead. When you start a project, do you think several moves ahead? Can you see potential in most things, even if your mates think you're mad at times? Do you imagine yourself running a big company or do you ever 'see' your photo in the pages of the *Financial Times*?

3. Sicko status: Can you keep going even when you're feeling out of sorts? Are you full of energy most days? Do you take care of your health by eating properly and exercising? Can you shrug off bugs like a cold? There's no taking time off work for sickies when you're your own boss!

4. Cool cucumber cred: You'll need to be able to stay calm. No tantrums, tears or depression unless absolutely necessary! What are you like in a panic? Can you keep a cool head when everyone else is flapping? Do you ever make a drama out of a crisis? Can you keep everyone cheered up and motivated? Do you ever blub for effect or can you keep any tears for quieter moments alone? Can you control your own temper and make sure you never lose it?

5. A mule mind: Like this animal you'll need a stubborn streak. If you keep getting put off by doom-mongers you'll never get anywhere. Can you stick to your guns when you know you're right? If someone disagrees with you can you negotiate calmly and clearly without backing down? If things aren't going your way, can you remotivate yourself, making sure you don't run out of steam and give your next shot a really good try?

6. Funny bones: Keeping your sense of humour will mean keeping yourself motivated and positive. Can you make yourself laugh or cheer yourself up when things aren't working? Can you see the funny side of most things?

7. An inner superhero: Bravery under fire is vital but so is having the guts to tell your negative inner voice where to go when it starts to sound wimpish. Are you able to give yourself a good talking to when necessary? You don't need to be brave all the time, but can you pull bravery out of the bag when you need to? Can you stop yourself worrying by focusing on the positives?

8. Creative juices: The ability to think differently is what makes for business brilliance. Do you tend to question everything? Do you think in a quirky way? When someone tells you the 'best' way to do something, do you ever think of an even better way?

9. Ears for it: Soak up the lot, listening with your eyes as well as your ears. Sometimes body language tells you more than words. Do you like watching people and trying to work out what they're thinking or what makes them tick? Are you able to focus on a conversation and listen to everything everyone else is saying? Do you often spot clues about another person's character that your mates seem to have missed? Can you guess what someone else is thinking before they say it? Are you good at sussing out someone's mood?

10. An eye for it: Great ideas are only part of the process. You should also be able to deal with smaller things like keeping to time, checking for spelling mistakes in emails or adverts. Are you good at concentrating on important things or can you drag your mind back to a piece of work when you start to get bored or distracted?

11. Keeping it real: Millionaire entrepreneurs tend to have simple ideas and simple solutions. Are you down to earth? Can you explain things simply and make them sound easy?

12. Enthusing it or losing it: Enthusiasm is as contagious as the flu. If you're keen about your idea or product, other people will be too. Do you get excited by new ideas, and can you keep that excitement going?

13. Tongue talent: You should be able to get your ideas and messages across to other people. Persuading and influencing skills are important too: you'll need to be good at winning people round. Are you good at talking? Are you happy to tell people your opinions and ask for things you want? Are you flexible? Can you change your tactics when you're trying to get your own way? Can you get other people to change their mind without getting into an argument?

14. Energy vibes: It inspires you and it inspires others. When you arrive in a room do people know you're there? Do you tend to move and walk quickly? Do your prefer action and movement to sitting and getting bored? Are you a bit of a fidget?

Improving Your Entrepreneur DNA – Quick Tips

1. Goal focus: This is easy and mostly a matter of discipline. All you have to do is imagine the best outcome for every job you do. Get into the habit of seeing what success looks like to you. Ask yourself what you want and what you want to happen before you get to work. You can even try this with simple jobs, like phoning a friend. Imagine what you want to happen as a result of your call. Do you want to cheer him/her up? Make them laugh? Get them to help you? Arrange a meeting? Knowing your ideal outcome will help you get the best results from anything. It helps to write goals down too or stick up pictures of anything you're trying to get, from a new bike to a house in the country.

2. Having the vision: Thinking big is all a matter of practice. Usually your mind will deal with the smaller stuff in life, but it's good to daydream about bigger goals as well. Plan some 'daydream' time in your day, maybe first thing in the morning or before you go off to sleep. 'Big vision' thinking helps to focus your mind on big goals as well as on small ones.

3. Keeping fit: Start your healthy lifestyle today. There's no need to get manic, just take a few minutes to look at how much you exercise and eat. Decide what you'd like to do to get fit and increase your energy levels. Make some sensible choices about junk food, snacks, late nights, smoking and alcohol. Remember, you're thinking long term here. Make some simple lifestyle commitments and stick to them. No cheating!

4. Tackle emotions: They're natural and without them you'd be weird. It's easier than you think to keep the negative ones in check when you want to keep cool. The first two steps are easy. When you think you're about to lose it:

(a) Take a break. Stop speaking. Pause. Make a gap.

(b) Go somewhere else. Get out of the room, away from the problem. If you can't, try to make a mind-gap by thinking of something else, something you like.

5. Talk to yourself: If things go wrong, listen to your inner voice. Is it telling you to give up? Is it saying you were stupid to have tried in the first place? Does it let you know you're never, ever lucky about anything? If so, stop listening. Tell it to shut up and bring out a better voice. Listen to the voice that tells you that wasn't failure, just one attempt that didn't work. Let it tell you what you can go on to try that might work. Tell yourself to keep going. There are only two types of failure: not trying or giving up.

6. Have a laugh: When you feel your sense of humour running for the door, try to kick-start it. Write down silly jokes you like. Keep a stock of DVDs of your favourite comedy shows or cartoons. Get in touch with friends who make you happy, not the ones who tend to make you listen to all their woes!

7. Hero-thinking: Brave thinking is all a state of mind: you're as good at it as anyone else. Get into that frame of mind by doing some inspirational reading. Hero-thinking is catching. Get stuck into autobiographies of anyone you admire and sit back and be inspired.

8. Use brain-teasers: They are a good way to grow an eye for detail. Visual quiz books are great because they help you to spot little details. Start with those 'Spot the difference' puzzles and build up to more complicated ones.

9. Simplifying things: It's easy! Pick out a book that is very wordy and complicated. Take a few paragraphs and translate each one into simple, concise, easy-to-understand language.

10. Be enthusiastic: Take a moment to think about things you like and things you like to do. How much time do you spend looking forward to them? How excited do you allow yourself to get? Do you remember to tell other people how much you enjoy doing them? Do you remember to tell yourself?

11. Work on talking skills: Start at least one conversation every day. If you can't think of anything to say, ask people about themselves. Ask a teacher about something they've told you in lesson. Try putting an opposing view across when you're chatting to friends, but without causing an argument. Respect their views of something, like a film, TV programme or bit of music, but share your own views too.

12. Do an instant energy makeover: Take ten seconds to pull yourself up to full height, breathe in deeply, then out again slowly. Give your shoulders and hands a small shake to relax them. Walk off with pace and energy, but without rushing.

MILLI-MOUTH

❝I wish the government would train kids to be more entrepreneurial.**❞** – *Alexander Amosu, nicknamed 'Lord of the Ringtones' after setting up RnB Ringtones, which turned over £1.2 million in its first year.*

How Your Money Works

Whatever you decide to do, you'll need a basic understanding of how money works. King Midas wished that everything he touched would turn into gold so that he could become the richest man in the world. When his wish came true, he begged to have his power taken away again because even his food and drink turned into shiny metal.

Of course, the point of this story is a good one: money has to be treated with respect, not worshipped. No business can run without it, so it's important to understand a few financial facts of life: above all, how to save money, how to earn it and how to work it.

MILLI-FACT

Special one million pound notes are used inside the Bank of England to save on space, but they never leave the bank. You wouldn't be very popular using one in the local newsagent's anyway – think of all that change!

First one of the world's top financial gurus has a few pointers.

HOT SEAT:
ALVIN HALL

Fast facts . . .

Who: *Alvin is a TV money expert who specializes in advising people on how to manage their cash.*

Success factor: *Alvin is from a poor American farming background, but he turned himself into a top financial adviser on Wall Street. He has presented BBC's* Your Money or Your Life *and written books packed with advice, like* You and Your Money.

Trivia bite: *His first purchase as a kid was two pieces of flashy luggage to take to summer school, which he saved up to buy.*

Do you think some people are born entrepreneurs?

I think there is an entrepreneurial gene. Most children probably don't have it, but if they do it tends to start showing itself at about 12 to 13 years old. It's not about making money so much as seeing the wonder of opportunities.

What are the best ways to save money?

I have never believed that children should be paid for doing things that are a natural part of being in the family, like tidying their rooms or laying the table. But it's OK to have a list up on the refrigerator for other kinds of chores, with what they're worth, like cleaning the car or the windows. Little jobs for neighbours are a good idea, as is tutoring other children or babysitting.

How should you manage your spending?

I'm a big believer in a concept I call 'scaffolding': half your money goes into savings and half goes on what you want. Spend and save is the message. It's important to understand the value of money.

What kinds of business ideas suit young people best?

Personally I don't think children should be doing exploitative things. I mean, things where you don't have to put much effort in, like simply buying things cheaply and selling them at a mark up. I think things where children have thought a bit out of the box are better. I know someone called Scott who made $12,000 just from investing in a company called Scott Paper because he liked the name. And I know three children who decided that they loved Cadbury's chocolate so much that they bought shares in the company.

What sort of investments are a good idea?

Between about 7 and 10, your parents should have opened a savings account for you. Keep things simple into your teens. Shares are probably not the way to go because they're complicated. Unit trusts (a safer option where someone else manages your investment) may be an option.

Who should you trust with your money?

If you do choose to set up a business, then it's important to tell your parents what you're doing. Your parents can help you. In the same way as a brilliant young piano player needs to be guided, so do young entrepreneurs.

MILLI-FACT

Sixty per cent of children either save all their pocket money or more than they spend throughout the year, according to a study by the Halifax bank.

Save It: How to Squirrel Away Cash

Before you can do anything interesting, especially to start a business, you need some money. And the more you save, the more you'll have to spend. Remember that old saying: 'Look after the pennies and the pounds will look after themselves'. Here are some top tips to double your money. Try thinking of your own too.

Fun ways to save

1. Buy posh on the cheap: People give away the most amazing things. Rather than buying new clothes or gadgets, check out charity shops for second-hand gear – especially in posh areas of town.

2. Make it up: Surprise friends and relatives with birthday cards and presents that you made yourself. They'll be pleased to get something unique that obviously took some effort. Cash in on your hobbies and make them work for you. For instance, you could burn a CD of their favourite hits, run up your own clothes, knit them a hot-water bottle cover or even cook up some delicious chocolate brownies.

3. Be a discount diva: Don't mind a scratch on something or a minor flaw in an item of clothing? Point it out and ask for a discount. You won't always get it, but if you don't ask you certainly won't. Expect ten per cent off. Always ask for special discounts for students. Even if shops and attractions don't offer them normally, they may be willing to make an exception.

4. Fashion passion: If you have a quick delve inside all those little shift dresses, tops and skirts that you're buying from high-street chains, you'll find they're cheap and easy to run up. And you might even find it turns out to be your big idea, designing and selling your own styles. You could save up to half the price of shop-bought items. At four dresses a year, you'd save around £80. Many fashion designers and retailers started this way.

5. Snack attack: Cutting out two packs of crisps per day, you'll save about £219 per year. And since it takes around 2–5 minutes to eat each bag, you'll gain an extra 36.5 hours per year too. This means you'd have time to learn a new skill, like computer graphics or practise scoring penalties.

6. Pool your games: If you buy computer games, form a pool with like-minded mates. Or form a larger group and contact the games manufacturers to offer your services as sample testers.

7. Bank it: Piggy banks are so last century. Open a real bank account. Usually, by the time you're 7 you're legally allowed to manage it yourself. Watch as the miracle of 'compound interest' kicks in on a savings account – scientist Albert Einstein called it 'the greatest mathematical discovery of all time'.

It works like this. In return for letting them look after your savings, a bank will pay you interest. This is usually paid at the end of the year. So at the end of the second year, you will receive interest on the first year's interest. Over the years, if left untouched, your savings could snowball as interest is paid on the interest on the interest . . . For example, if you put £1,000 in a savings account and leave it there for ten years at an interest rate of 5 per cent, you'd end up with £1,629 without adding any more of your own money. If you fancy being more adventurous, ask your parents to investigate what are called unit trusts. These are stock market investments that they can open for you.

MILLI-FACT

Cracker-crazy Julian Reed saved his family cash by making his first box of homemade festive bangers at 13. He now runs a million-pound firm called Robin Reed, selling ten million Christmas crackers all over the planet.

Wild and Wacky Ways to Save

1. Freebie frenzy: You'd be surprised where you can get free goodies. Why go to Starbucks when you can get coffee for free from a machine in your local bank?

2. Present and collect: Before birthdays and Christmas, surf the Internet using price-comparison sites to save the whole family money.

3. Save on cosmetics: Going to a party? Then pop into your local department store and ask for a free makeover. Even boys can try out the new spot creams for free.

4. Design your own entertainment: Create cartoon stories of your mates, draw cards or start a student magazine. It's fun and you can sell them at a low price to cover costs. You'll learn great branding, design and marketing skills along the way.

5. See shows for free: A lot of TV and radio programmes, from quiz shows to sitcoms, get in live audiences and you don't have to pay to be in them. Apply to the BBC or ITV for tickets. This will also show you what goes on behind the scenes, which will help your rise to success in the media industry. See *www.bbc.co.uk/whatson/tickets* or *www.tickets.granadamedia.com* for example.

6. Keep wild pets . . . instead of tame ones. Nature provided us with birds, mice, rats and foxes outside your home. The good thing is, you don't have to buy food or clean them out (although a garden vole might object to being dressed up in bling like one of Paris Hilton's pooches).

Working It: Money-Awareness for Beginners

Millionaires are always very money-aware. No, they don't sit in attics with a moth-eaten moggie for company, counting coins by the light of a candle and waiting for a visit from the Ghost of Christmas Past. But they do keep track of their dosh. So if your idea of financial-awareness is rattling the piggy bank up against your ear, you'll need to read through these tips pronto!

1. Keep a dosh diary: Write down everything you spend and earn in a week. You might be surprised at the results! It's good to know how your costs add up. Are they more or less than the money coming in? Is there a profit left or do you end up with a loss? Are there ways of saving more to pay for things you really want?

2. Push the profit: If you're in profit at the end of the week, spend time thinking of ways to increase that profit margin. How could you make more dosh each week? How could you cut down on your spending?

3. Keep track of any savings: If you have a bank or savings account, start to keep track of the interest. Find out what interest you're getting and check how competitive it is. You don't even need to have real savings to learn all about interest and investments. Have a 'virtual' account competition with a friend. Agree on a sum, say £500, in each account, and see who can earn the most with it. Study the financial pages of a newspaper and invest the money – perhaps in savings or in stocks and shares. It's a fun and painless way to get to know how finances work. Remember, though, because the money isn't real it's easy to take big risks. When you're investing the real thing, such risks could have more painful consequences.

4. Learn before you try: Try skimming the financial pages of your daily newspaper. Learn to tell your Dow Jones from your Hang Seng. If you get a taste for it, try financial websites or reading through the *Financial Times*.

5. Practise haggling: You won't get rich settling for the first price on anything. Try it out at the local market or car-boot sale. Haggling just means negotiating a price when you want to buy or sell something. It takes confidence, so the sooner you try the quicker you'll learn the skills without feeling awkward. Many shops are willing to drop a price by asking 'Is that your best price?' Try haggling with friends too. If you have something they want, like a CD, try bartering for something they have that you'd like.

6. Log your skills: What are you good at and how much could that skill be worth? Brainstorm skill ideas, taking a large sheet of paper and writing down all your skills, regardless of whether you think you're good or not. When you're at school you'll be with people who probably have the same skills as you, but did you realize that many of those skills could be much rarer and worth money when you start work? Try to avoid taking your skills for granted. Can you do graphics or use specialized programs on your computer? Are you artistic or literary? All skills can be developed into something that could create long-term success.

BANK ON THIS
Where to Put Your Money

★ Lots of banks offer accounts to under-18s with really good rates of interest, which means you end up with more than you started with. These are a good way to save. Shop around for the best rates.

★ After the age of 8 you can have an account in your own name and make deposits and withdrawals yourself. Once you're over 16 accounts usually come with a cashpoint card and a cheque book. Look out for free gifts when you open an account. Fortunately no one will give you an overdraft until you are 18, so you can't go bust!

★ You have probably heard of buying shares on the stock market. When you buy a share you are buying a tiny share of a company. The value of shares can go up and down, so it's a risky business. Under-18s can't buy shares, but their parents can on their behalf – by setting up a trust. There are even tax benefits to be had. If you're interested, talk to your parents about it.

Earn It: Start Making Some Money

Saving will only get you so far. Increase your savings by earning some cash. Here are some easy ways to kick off your finances.

1. Be job wise: Getting a job needn't be boring. Like horses? Try the stables. Like sports? Caddy at a golf course. Even if it's boring, your income is near 100 per cent profit. Unlike adults, you probably don't have to worry about paying a mortgage or rent. Part-time jobs look good on your CV and will impress employers at interviews.

2. Odd jobs: There's no limit to the chores that other people don't want to do, like washing their cars or sweeping their drive. This is where you come in!

3. Pet sitting: Your parents might think you're still too young to babysit. But what about pet sitting or dog walking? Taking care of the neighbour's hamster while they're away could be the ideal way for the cash to paw in.

4. Grow it on trees: Start growing fruit and veg. Then set up a stall at school or at the front of your house to sell them.

5. Be competitive: Enter as many free competitions as you can in newspapers and on telly. Some have age limits, but many don't. Win a *Blue Peter* badge to get into attractions more cheaply.

6. Sell old stuff: Fashions change, gadgets go out of date. Don't throw them away. Persuade your parents to help you do a car-boot sale or sell things on eBay. What you don't want someone else will. Believe it or not, wigmakers even pay for old hair.

7. Capitalize on your skills: Good swimmer? Think about training to become a part-time lifeguard.

8. Become a consultant: You *have* got special skills. Make use of them. For instance, you probably know more about green issues than older people. Offer to help save a relative or friend's energy bill by pointing out where they could turn off gadgets on standby or use 'green' lightbulbs. You could offer to do a green audit for them. If they appreciate the help, ask them to pass your details on to friends or neighbours. Ask for a small fee for doing the same for them.

BANK ON THIS
Work This Out if You Want a Part-Time Job

1. The green light news: you can get a part-time job once you're 13, but it can't be in a factory or anywhere else you shouldn't be, like a pub.

2. Before you're 15 you must not work for more than 25 hours a week. As a 15-year-old you must not work for more than 35 hours a week. There are lots more laws on what you are allowed to do and you need to check them at *www.direct.gov.uk*

3. There are no set rules about the minimum age to start your own business (though you'll need help to do it formally).

easyJet founder Stelios is one of the best-known entrepreneurs on the planet, but even he had other plans for his life when he was at school . . .

HOT SEAT:
SIR STELIOS HAJI-IOANNOU

Fast facts

Who: *The brains behind low-cost airline easyJet and countless other easyGroup brands, including car rental, cruises and pizza.*
Success factor: *Born in Greece, he founded easyJet in 1995 and, according to* The Sunday Times Rich List, *was worth £1.29 billion in 2006.*
Trivia bite: *Stelios was knighted for his services to entrepreneurship in 2006.*

As a child, did you want to be an entrepreneur? If so, what age did you start coming up with business ideas?

As a child I wanted to be a footballer! But then I had a formal business education and joined the family shipping firm. A couple of years later I realized that I wanted to be my own boss, so at the age of 25 I founded my own shipping firm, Stelmar (as in Stelios Maritime) Shipping. That business listed on the New York Stock Exchange in 2001 and was sold to another shipping company in 2005 for approximately $1.3 billion. I was 28 when I founded easyJet.

What attracted you to business?

I think I was always destined for a career in business. My father is a self-made man who sometimes worked from home, so I was brought up to the sound of him on the telephone running his business affairs. I then had a formal business education at the London School of Economics and the City University Business School. So both my upbringing and my education indicated that I would work in business as opposed to other professional areas.

How did you get the idea for easyJet? Was there a 'moment of inspiration'?

I think it was more a process of inspiration rather than a sudden moment. Even after I had set up my own shipping business I was still trying to shake off the 'daddy's boy' image. My father made his fortune in shipping, so I guess I didn't want people to think I had only made it because of him. In the early 1990s I met Richard Branson, one of my business heroes, who offered me a franchise in his airline, Virgin Atlantic, running the London to Athens route. Fortunately I declined, as that particular franchise later went bust, but I think I caught the aviation bug off Sir Richard. I then flew Southwest Airlines, the godfather of all low-cost carriers, on a trip to the States and the idea began to gel. The airline industry in Europe was just beginning to deregulate at that time, opening doors to competition and non-state owned airlines. So I founded easyJet and the rest is history.

What attitude helped you get where you are?

Determination and perseverance help a lot. When I came to the UK and started easyJet, many people thought I wouldn't succeed and some of them even told me so. You have to keep on trying, different methods if needs be. And it's still like that, with all the 16 businesses in the easyGroup. Forgive the pun, but it's not all easy going in business!

Did you ever find age a problem?

Absolutely, and it is only thanks to my father's wealth that I was able to get into both shipping and aviation while I was still in my twenties. They are both asset-heavy and expensive industries to get into and my father lent me the money, where no bank would have lent to a relatively inexperienced and young person. But not all industries are so capital-intensive. The Internet particularly has provided the opportunity for people to set up businesses that are less capital-intensive.

How would you advise young people to finance their ideas?

If possible, get yourself a rich father! But I realize that may not be available to everyone and there are sources of funding beyond banks alone. So-called 'business angels', often individuals, can fund small businesses and the next rung up the ladder, in terms of quantity of money, are venture capitalists. If you have a more mature business in need of large amounts of capital for expansion, there are stock markets and private equity funds.

What was your biggest setback and how did you deal with it?

During the dotcom bubble at the end of the 1990s and the beginning of this millennium, conventional business rules seem to be suspended. So long as you had an Internet-related business which was growing and had customers, banks, suppliers and even stock markets would give you money without really worrying about your profitability. So I grew my chain of Internet cafes much faster than is sensible for what was basically a high-street retail business – 22 giant stores in 9 countries over 2 continents in 18 months! When the dotcom bubble burst I realized that I had some big costs in the business, so I paid off creditors and concentrated on the core competence of the business – cheap, fast and efficient Internet access for the public at large. It paid off, as there are now about three times as many easyInternet cafe outlets than there were five years ago, but they are in smaller, less expensive locations and they focus on what consumers really want.

What luxury do you spoil yourself with?

My one remaining luxury is, I think, my boat that I use in the Mediterranean very infrequently these days. I guess all Greeks with a shipping legacy have their own private yacht! Otherwise, I don't really have any luxuries which are out of the ordinary. The only car that I drive myself is a Smart car. I wear an easyWatch and I dress from the usual high-street stores, often their branches at airports.

Which area of business should young people target?

I think that depends upon the individual. If I had not been fortunate enough to have a wealthy father to bankroll my early ventures, I think I would have started a kebab shop. Who knows, it might have been a chain of kebab shops by now! But the Internet does still have lots of possibilities too and, as I said, it has the advantage of not needing to be capital-intensive, at the early stages at least.

What is the secret of your success?

It's not really a secret. Hard work, determination and an ability to make decisions have all helped me, but then so too has luck!

How do you stop it going to your head?

Again, that's up to the individual, but I like to think that success is a journey, not a destination. Try not to think that you've made it at any specific time because that's when you might get complacent or, as you say, let it go to your head.

Where do you do your best thinking?

Travelling, and keeping your ears and eyes open, is what helps me to try to spot trends, developments and what might be the next opportunity. Travelling, meeting and talking to people are the catalysts that start me thinking about what I could do next.

STELIOS'S TOP TIPS

★ Work hard. Sorry if that sounds obvious or even boring, but you often get out of something as much as you are prepared to put in in the first place.

★ Try to have fun. If you're having fun the hard work doesn't seem so hard. Most of the businesses I have started were hobbies of mine in one form or another, so I can genuinely enjoy myself when I am at work.

★ Make your own decisions. Help and advice are great if you can get it and afford it, but anyone who is running their own business has to be able to make the final decision. Study it and think about it, but sometimes you just have to follow your own gut instinct.

Be Inspired

So you've got an idea of what entrepreneur DNA is all about, as well as ways of managing your cash, but how do you get the inspiration and motivation you'll need to get a business or big project off the ground?

Stelios was lucky enough to have a minted dad, but what if your parents are skint or reluctant to part with the cash? Is it possible to start up in business with just the small change in your pocket?

Here's a business dynamo who reckons you can turn your passion into a successful business without huge amounts of money.

HOT SEAT:
EMMA HARRISON

Fast facts

Who: *One of Britain's top female entrepreneurs.*

Success factor: *Founder of the training agency A4e, she's worth around £55 million.*

Trivia bite: *Went undercover to clean toilets for Channel 4's Secret Millionaire, looking for someone deserving to share a chunk of her fortune.*

Were you interested in business at school and was being an entrepreneur a thing you were encouraged to do?

We didn't have much money when I was a child and so I ran illegal tuck shops at school to make myself some. I learnt important business lessons that way.

There was no encouragement to become an entrepreneur. In fact it was the opposite. I wanted to be an engineer, but I was told that if I became an engineer no one would marry me. It was nonsense. The encouragement I had came from my father.

What do you wish you'd been told back then?

I wish someone had told me that it was possible to go into business on your own. It felt like we were all being trained up to be corporate fodder. There should be more encouragement in schools with enterprise schemes and entrepreneurs visiting them to tell children about what it's like.

What's the most important lesson a future entrepreneur can learn?

If there's something you are passionate about you should go for it. You can make money and a life out of it. You need to have a sense of purpose. I was a clever girl at school and so I was pushed into becoming a doctor, but what no one realized was that I couldn't stand the sight of blood. The result was that I failed all my A levels. But it was the best thing that could have happened to me. Underneath I had all this entrepreneurial stuff going on, organizing parties and running tuck shops, but no one valued that, they just thought I was being naughty.

What made you realize that business could be for you?
I got myself back to college and into a job, but I realized that a nine-to-five lifestyle wasn't for me. I thought, there must be something better than this, so an opportunity came along to run my dad's small training business and I took the plunge.

Is it possible to have an ethical approach to business and make money?
Money gives you choice. Lack of money means a lack of opportunity. But my philosophy is 'doing well by doing good'. The really successful entrepreneurs don't talk about the money, they talk about wanting to make something better. Those that just want to make a big load of money will invariably fail.

How would you advise young people to get started?
Talk about what you want to do and show people your plans. No one is going to suddenly come and find you in your bedroom. If you're prepared to go out there with your idea, someone may be prepared to invest in it. You don't need loads of money to start up. In fact starting at a low level may be the best way. It's all about networking and contacts. Get a mentor – because they may end up investing in your idea.

What's the difference between someone in business and an entrepreneur?

It's important to distinguish. Someone who runs a business may not be suited to being an entrepreneur, who is someone who creates a business. I have 2,000 people working for me and lots of them are better at 'running a business' than I could ever be.

What's the silliest business idea you ever came across?

There are some crazy business people around. There was one girl I knew who had put £40,000 into an idea and she came and saw me and I told her it wouldn't work. Her house was at risk and everything. It's important to listen to those with experience and communicate your ideas well. If you can't put your concept into a couple of sentences, then you probably don't have a clear idea of what it is yourself.

What dream has your success allowed you to fulfil?

I live in a stately home with loads of my mates from school and we share everything. We always talked about doing it when we were young and now our dream has come true.

What's your final message to young entrepreneurs of the future?

Get out there and start. Learn by making mistakes. Do nothing and you will get nowhere. Do something and you have got half a chance of success.

Finding the Inspirational Buzz

Knowing what inspires you in life is vital if you're going to be a happy and successful entrepreneur. Inspiration gives you energy, drive and determination, plus the motivation to keep going when things aren't going well. So what exactly inspires you?

Inspiration can come from many sources and we're all completely different when it comes to our own special buzz. You could be inspired by a story, film, book or TV series. A famous person could inspire you, but so could a friend, cousin or next-door neighbour. You could be inspired by the idea of helping others or even the thought of paying others to work for you. Praise from a teacher or parent might inspire you, but so could criticism or being told you'll never do well. A person can be as inspired to prove a critic wrong as work to prove them right.

BRAIN BOX

Investigate Your Inspiration Factor by Doing This Simple Test

★ Write down your biggest achievements so far. Underneath each one write down what inspired you to do it.

★ Was it the thought of a reward? Did you think of someone you admired who'd achieved great things? Did you work to get praise or approval from someone you respected? Were you offered a treat or cash? Did you do it to make someone else happy or was it prompted by the fear of doing badly? Did you want to compete with someone and win, or did you want to please yourself?

★ Then underneath each inspirational factor write down exactly how it made you feel at the time. What emotion did it/they create in you? Were there any other factors? (For instance, you might say your mother inspired you by encouraging you to study for an exam. But if you think longer you might also remember that you were also inspired by a brother or sister rivalry or even jealousy of a friend who'd done well at something else.)

★ Keep all those thoughts and emotions in mind next time you want to achieve something special.

Discover what gives you that buzz of excitement and inspiration, rather than something that other people think you should be doing. Go with your heart as well as your mind. Success comes in many shapes and sizes. Just make sure you get the right fit for you.

Here's how one teenage tycoon got his inspiration.

HOT SEAT:
FRASER DOHERTY

Fast facts

Who: *A brilliant young entrepreneur who has managed to turn jam-making into a thriving business.*

Success factor: *He started his business, SuperJam, at 14, using his grandmother's secret recipe. He now runs Doherty Preserves, supplying orders all over the globe. Check out www.jamshop.co.uk*

Trivia bite: *He started with just £2.*

Did you always want to be an entrepreneur?

I would say that I was eccentric even as a child and I always had little 'projects' on the go. I used to sell sweets in the playground. I sold bacon and sausages door to door and did odd jobs for the neighbours. One time I got a box of eggs from a farm and kept them warm on the cable box under the TV. Three weeks later, four chicks hatched and I kept them in the garden until they started laying eggs, which I sold to the neighbours. Sadly, the chickens were eaten by a fox after a year or so and I had to move on to the next hare-brained idea.

I suppose I was born an entrepreneur but I didn't necessarily relate that to running my own business until I was a teenager. For ages I wanted to work for Greenpeace and I used to sell things to raise money for them, which was entrepreneurial but in a different way compared to what I do now.

In an age of computer fortunes, what made you think that jam could have such potential?

I think it is important to start a business doing something that you love. Some people are crazy about music, so start a music shop or sell musical instruments, other people like computers and start businesses designing them, for example. It's a bit of a mad thing to be passionate about, but I love jam and eat it maybe four times every day, so naturally I started a business selling jam. Jam hasn't changed much in centuries and I was certain that I wanted to be the one to totally reinvent how people think about jam, what they do with it, how it tastes and what it does to their body. I spent ages coming up with the idea for SuperJam, which is essentially a range of jams that are made entirely from fruit and are therefore far better tasting and more nutritious than what is otherwise available. The fact that I was entering a declining market that has been around for centuries and is dominated by massive food companies was part of the challenge and added something to the thrill of it all.

How did you go about funding and researching your business ideas and what advice would you give to other young entrepreneurs?

I started my business one day after visiting my gran when she was making jam. She showed me her secret recipe and I ran round to the supermarket and bought some fruit, sugar and a plastic bucket. I made a few jars of jam that day and, before they had even cooled down properly, started knocking on the neighbours' doors, offering them a free jar of my homemade jam. When I went back the next week, all of the neighbours bought a few jars of jam and I realized that my idea was going to take off. I just worked really hard from that point and now have contracts to supply some of the biggest retailers in the country.

I think a lot of young people imagine that it costs a lot of money to start a business and that they need to know lots about business.

I started my business with £2, some imagination and a lot of hard work and there's no reason to say that anyone reading this book couldn't do the same.

Was there anything that made it difficult to be taken seriously as a teenage businessman?
Understandably, adults tend to have reservations about doing business with teenagers. I had absolutely no experience or money when I was starting out; just an idea and an ambition to reinvent jam. Not everyone took me seriously when I first met them, but I made a point of proving to them that I was just as capable as anyone else of doing what I had set out to do.

When you are a teenager trying to do something as ambitious as supplying the major supermarkets, you have to prove to everyone around you that even though you are a totally inexperienced teenager, you have what it takes to achieve your goal. Everything you do, every email you write, every phone call you make and every meeting that you hold has got to be very professional. You have to remove any doubt in their mind about your ability.

It is also crucial to be totally honest and open with everyone that you deal with. Ask for everyone's advice and listen to what they say. Most people will be happy to help you if they like you, trust you and believe in your idea too.

What I have found is that my age has been by biggest asset in developing my business. It has led to a lot of media coverage of my story and has helped SuperJam to stand out from other jam brands.

You have said that one of the benefits of your success was meeting celebrities. Who were you most in awe of and who do you look up to in the business world?
I haven't really met many celebrities who I have been in awe of, but it was pretty cool having tea at 11 Downing Street and going on Richard Hammond's *Five o'clock Show*, for example. I don't have

any heroes who I have pictures of on my bedroom wall or anything like that, but I admire people like Warren Buffet (investor), Ingvar Kamprad (Ikea) and Steve Jobs (Apple computers). I am quite happy to do my own thing in life, though, rather than trying to emulate anyone else's success.

What has been your biggest setback?

It took about a year of full-time work by myself and others to develop the SuperJam recipes, packaging and production. It took so long because we would develop a range of products and send them to the supermarkets for their feedback. They didn't like the first few attempts and it was quite hard going being rejected after months of work. Dozens of label designs and recipes had to be thrown in the bin.

What makes running my own business so enjoyable for me is the fact that it is so difficult. New obstacles pop up every day and the satisfaction comes from being able to overcome them.

What kind of music motivates you?

My favourite band is probably The Smiths but I have maybe ten thousand songs on my iPod, which contains rock, folk, jazz and all sorts. I like music a lot and go out to see live music a couple of times a week, which is quite a nice way to relax after a day of jam selling. Listening to music kept me going when I was stirring pots of jam 16 hours a day, seven days a week.

Do you want to be a millionaire?

Making heaps of money is not at all what running my own business is about for me. I run my own business for the challenge and thrill of it, not because I want to buy a big car or a big house. I suppose that I would like to be a millionaire in the sense that it would be proof that I was good at what I am doing. If I do become wealthy, then I would like to do good with my wealth. I would get a lot more joy out of building an orphanage than I would from buying a Ferrari.

What are your future business plans?

I have dozens of new business ideas every day, most of them totally mad. With SuperJam, I hope to supply all of the major UK supermarkets and probably also expand abroad at some point. I'm working on some new recipes and planning various promotions to encourage people to try my jam over the coming year. I will be launching SuperJam in 180 Waitrose supermarkets in March 2007, which is what I am currently working towards.

FRASER'S TOP TIPS

★ **Money doesn't make you rich:** For me, the most important thing is that acquiring spectacular wealth isn't at the top of my lifetime 'to do' list. I am running my own business because I enjoy every minute of it and I think that this outlook makes it much easier when things aren't going well. If I went bankrupt tomorrow I wouldn't be too worried because I have enjoyed the experience of running my own business so much and would love to start all over and do it again.

★ **Do what you want in life:** I think that the best careers advice that I could possibly give to someone reading this is to be wary of people giving them careers advice. There will be people around you telling you to go for the safe option of getting a job in an office. If that doesn't feel like what you want to do with your life, you have got to ignore them.

★ **Be different:** For a lot of young people, there is a fear of standing out. I've never cared what my peers have thought of me. Lots of kids laughed at me when I started selling jam or raised chickens in my garden, but I wasn't put off.

An entrepreneur is somebody who starts something, so by now you should be thinking about exciting projects. Keep these points in mind as you move on to thinking about just what that big idea might be.

★ Learn about money – how to value it, make it, save it and how to respect it.

★ You don't need huge amounts of money to start something.

★ The key to success isn't focusing on dreams of dosh but improving or starting something brilliant.

★ Think out of the box – entrepreneurial ideas can cover every area of life.

3.
LEARN TO BE A BRILLIAN-AIRE

You've thought about your strengths and skills and looked at improving those skills and developing your confidence to help you create success. Now, how are you going to cash in on your unique selling points?

Your next step is to take all your skills and enthusiasm and concentrate on an idea that will use them the most. Great business ideas can be simple, so you won't necessarily need to wait until something big and complex springs to mind.

The good thing is that you already know most of the gaps in the market. Think how many things you do during the day that are awkward or inconvenient. Or how many things you need or want that just aren't in the shops yet. Does your computer do everything you want it to do? Look for areas of improvement or opportunity.

This chapter's going to point you in the right direction, to help you come up with your 'next big thing'. It will show you exercises and brain-training to get you to your own Eureka moment and it shares the thoughts of others who've turned their own great thoughts into huge successes.

MILLI-MOUTH

❝Business opportunities are like buses, there's always another one coming.❞ – *Richard Branson, boss of Virgin*

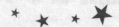

What's the Big Idea?

First, you can try working your own grey matter. A brain can be a bit like a car engine: you need to put the right fuel in and know how to make it run well. What makes your brain tick over best?

Imagine this: you decide it's your destiny to become a teen extraordinaire. All you need to set off on the path to super-sized success is one really stonking idea. So you sit down with a large sheet of paper and a pencil and you start to write a list of money-making wheezes. What do you think happens next?

(a) Within half an hour you've written so much your pencil is worn down to a stub?

or

(b) By the end of half an hour you're picking your nose with a paperclip and staring at a blank sheet of paper.

The sensible money's on the paperclip.

Your brain is a wonderful structure, but it is also something of a diva. It likes to work at its own pace and in its own way. Put pressure on it, by trying to have brilliant brainwaves, and it'll often throw a hissy fit and refuse to work properly at all.

If that's the case, where do those big ideas come from? Here's one of Britain's top inventors, who had his big idea while he was watching telly.

HOT SEAT:
TREVOR BAYLIS

Fast facts

Who: *The brains behind the world famous wind-up radio.*
Success factor: *After being featured on TV Trevor's radio became a hit in developing countries. Tens of thousands have since been sold.*
Trivia bite: *As well as being a top inventor, Trevor swam for Great Britain at 15 and once worked as a stunt man too.*

Were you inventing things as child?

I had a Meccano set which I loved. I was making things almost before I could read or write. My father was an engineer and he inspired me. By the time I was 14 I had made my own diesel engine. The secret to inventing is to have fun. Inventing is the future. You can change the world and make a few bob along the way too.

Where did you get the idea for the clockwork radio?

I was sat watching TV and there was a piece on the news about a terrible disease in Africa. People needed to be educated by radio about the risks. But there wasn't enough electricity or batteries. I had this flash, imagining myself as an old-fashioned traveller with a gramophone in the wilderness. They didn't have electricity then. I suddenly thought that it must be possible to get enough energy out of a spring to power a dynamo in a radio by simply winding it up.

Do you have to be brilliant at school to be a great inventor?

Achievement is more important than qualifications. I was a bit of a failure at school, but when I was in a workshop I loved playing around with ideas and making things. The important thing to remember is that invention is treasure. A paperclip is a simple thing, but we still use millions of them and it's never been bettered. It's all about coming up with solutions to problems. My advice is, follow your heart.

What should you do if you have a good idea?

It's important not to go round the playground telling everyone. It's a good idea to start researching it on the Internet first to see if it's already been done. Nine times out of ten it will have been, but maybe you'll have hit on something no one has thought of. Then you need to get in touch with the Patent Office and protect what is called your 'intellectual property'. Remember, no one pays you for a good idea. But they might pay you for a piece of paper that says you own the idea.

Where's a good place to work?

The garden shed, if you have one. You're probably going to need a prototype and this is a great place to tinker and avoid getting the house dirty. That's where I started work on my clockwork radio.

What makes a successful inventor?

You have to have a big ego and believe in yourself, because people will always be saying things can't be done. I always say that I don't mind people looking down on me as long as they don't expect me to be always looking up to them. A lot of people said my clockwork radio would never work at first. You're going to have loads of ideas that don't work, but you have to keep going.

Is there enough help out there for inventors?

My organization, Trevor Baylis Brands, helps inventors to get their ideas off the ground. See *www.trevorbaylisbrands.com*

It doesn't matter what age you are – anyone can be an inventor. We have to change the image of engineering too. Girls can be just as good as boys at it. It's not all about men with oily rags. There needs to be more help at school – someone there that you can trust to go to with your ideas.

What invention do you think the world needs most?

Global warming is the biggest problem facing us. If we could solve the problem of nuclear fission then we could get huge amounts of energy with not much input, and we wouldn't have to rely on fuels like coal or oil.

BANK ON THIS

Five People Whose Ideas Changed the World

Percy Spencer: He came up with the idea for the microwave oven when a chocolate bar in his pocket melted while he was working in a lab with microwave radio signals.

Mary Anderson: She invented the windscreen wiper in 1905. Ten years later they were standard for all cars.

Steve Jobs: He was the brains behind funky Apple computers and the iPod.

Art Fry: He thought of the Post-It note when he realized one day that sticky bits of paper would work better than ordinary bookmarks.

Scott Olson: He invented rollerblades. All right, so maybe they didn't change the world, but they're fun and they made their inventor a millionaire.

MILLI-FACT

Only 20 per cent of millionaire fortunes come
from inherited wealth.

Brain-training

To emerge with a truly mouth-droolingly magnificent business idea
or invention, you'll need to learn how to work your brain. Moments
of brilliance don't come to order and the more pressure you put on
those brain cells the more likely they are to shut all the doors and
turn out the lights. Think brain-training sounds hard? Don't worry,
it's not. You can work your brain any time and anywhere, even as
you're going off to sleep. It's all a case of knowing the right place
and right time, then creating the right conditions for your milli-thinking.

Top spots for good-quality thinking are:

1. The toilet. Funnily, this was numero uno with more guys than
   girls.
2. The bath. Avoid flushing your best ideas down the pan and let
   them bubble up during a relaxing soak.
3. In bed. It seems your grey cells love a lie-in just as much as
   you do!

Very few people seem to get those lightbulb-above-the head
moments while sitting at their desk.

BRAIN BOX 1
Big Thinking Tips

Warm up . . .

★ Clear the clutter. No, this isn't sponsored by mums across the land as a ruse to make you clean up your room. Clutter creates distraction.

★ Create calm. Sit somewhere quiet. In psychology terms you're aiming to get into what's called the relaxed, half-asleep state known as the alpha state. Only don't nod off!

★ Play music. Make it background stuff to avoid distraction.

★ Meditate. Close your eyes and allow your brain to wander

★ Take off your shoes. Relaxed feet mean relaxed mind.

★ Suck your thumb. Or any other self-comfort gesture that works for you.

★ Look up and to the right. If you don't want to close your eyes, this eye direction will stimulate creative thought.

★ Get bored. It's a good state to be in for big-ideas thinking.

★ Keep away from your computer screen. We're in a culture of constant busyness but the brain likes to work on one thing at a time. Don't sit at your computer fiddling and grazing while you think.

★ Keep a 'think' book. You never know when that great idea's going to hit you, so carry a notebook at all times to scribble it down before you forget.

★ Keep it big. Also try working on a huge piece of paper with big fat pens.

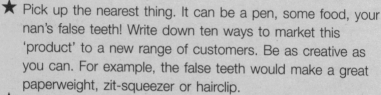

BRAIN BOX 2
Big Thinking Workouts

Do some trial 'idea' runs

★ Pick up the nearest thing. It can be a pen, some food, your nan's false teeth! Write down ten ways to market this 'product' to a new range of customers. Be as creative as you can. For example, the false teeth would make a great paperweight, zit-squeezer or hairclip.

★ List as many things as you can think of to do with a paperclip, as quickly as possible.* Now list things that you *can't* do with a paperclip.**

★ Using a newspaper or magazine, create the highest tower you can.

★ List ten things in your life that are inconvenient to do and invent a better way of doing each of them. For example, toilet seats up/down, the gunk left on your hands after using hair products, losing the remote control, computer cables, food stuck in the keyboard.

★ Create a new food outlet that would appeal to your age group, including menu with ideal prices, decor, music, etc. Sketch the plans and create a catchy name for it that would pull the customers in.

★ Or: design a new magazine that your age group would buy, including its size, price, title, contents and cost. List ideal advertisers that you could sell space to and come up with ideas for new and different features or format.

★ Imagine you're launching a new product – you! Think of ten different and original ways to make yourself high profile.

★ Sit with the following things or hobbies and create ways of selling them to a generation of trendy-types: jigsaws, train-spotting, big pants, bread crusts, hot-water bottles, nodding dogs, bath salts, jogging bottoms.

* The answer to this is; you can do anything with a paperclip, you just have to think creatively.
** If this list is longer than your Can Do list, you're not thinking creatively enough. Go back and try again!

The Eureka Moment

This is the name people use to describe the moment when you think of that really good idea or the solution to a problem.

How do you get your brain to come up with your own Eureka moment? Here are some tips:

1. Make sure you've got all the facts about your idea.
2. Move away from the problem or idea. If you've been picking your brains so clean they look like a turkey carcass the day after Boxing Day, stop sitting there puzzling and go out for a walk or something.
3. Or have a quick nap. Nap-style snoozing can help clear the brain of gunk and allow that idea to emerge.
4. Or daydream. Put your thinking on a different plain. Just don't go off for too long.

5. Or walk the dog, clear out your wardrobe, decorate your room – anything that keeps you in one place for some time while allowing your thoughts to wander.
6. Or soak in the bath (showers aren't so good for creating Eureka moments).

HOT SEAT:
OLIVER BRIDGE

Fast facts

Who: *Teenage tycoon who set up Bigger Feet:* www.biggerfeet.co.uk
Success factor: *Inspired by the lack of large shoes, he realized that there were one million people in the same boat. He started his own company in 2004, aged 15.*
Trivia bite: *Won the teen category at 2005's Enterprising Young Brits.*

Where did the idea for Bigger Feet come from?

I was on holiday in the Lake District, and was unable to find any size 13 walking boots. I was sitting in despair in the shoe shop when my mum said, 'Why don't you try and sell some?' That was the Eureka moment, and from then on I set about creating my own limited company to buy and sell large footwear. I realized there was massive demand that wasn't finding an outlet, and after a bit of research found out that there were only a few competitors: it looked like quite a safe bet.

Did you always dream of making it big in business?

From a young age I've been fascinated with money and had a virtual stock portfolio at the age of 10. Consequently, I had always fancied a job in the City or in finance, and so, yes, I suppose there was that desire to succeed in business. However, that was an abstract desire, and one which I was only able to specifically formulate once I had the idea for the shoe company.

What have been the hardest things about being so young and setting up a business?

Well, I was only 15 when the company was set up, so a family friend, Paul Wilkinson (age 43), who had recently started his own business, acted as my legal guarantor, co-signing all the company legal documents, tax forms, etc. The hardest bit has been the severity of the learning curve, and gaining the confidence to talk to adults on equal terms, although this has certainly developed as I have been forced into unenviable scenarios with account managers and the bank from time to time!! For instance, once I had to call our biggest suppliers to ask for a credit extension. This was a hard argument since the account manager knew I was only 16. Unsurprisingly, I failed to convince him, and I had to withdraw £500 from my savings to tide over the bank account until the cash flow improved.

How did you finance the start up of the business?

I have worked as a DJ for several years with a friend, and we do school parties and weddings – that provides a good income. With all my savings (I come from a saving-orientated family) and the disco income, I set it up myself, just hoping that I could make my money back!

Do you think more teenagers should aspire to become millionaire entrepreneurs?

Being an entrepreneur is great. You work for yourself with no one telling you what to do, you enjoy an exciting ride and all the profits are yours. However, everyone needs to realize that at the end of the day money is merely a means to an end. There is little point in having a million pounds if you've got no friends to enjoy it with. So, by all means, aspire to be a millionaire entrepreneur, but make sure you don't sacrifice too much to get there. Fortunately I have been able to strike a nice balance, and don't feel that there has been much of a trade off, but you have to be careful sometimes – you can become too wrapped up in your own business problems and neglect other, more important, areas of your life.

If you were going to splash out on a dream present for yourself, what would it be?

I suppose my dream present would be a nice yacht, one on which I could entertain my friends. We could go swimming, jet-skiing, drink fancy cocktails, etc.! However, although I have been to the Sun Seeker boat showroom in West London for a bit of fun, I think it is perhaps out of my price range at the moment! I have treated myself to a few new things – an iPod, a new stereo, an LCD monitor for my PC and the usual clothes and aftershave! However, I haven't really made enough profit (yet) to splash out too extravagantly!

You have said that 'switching off' is important. What do you do to relax?

Firstly, I like my sport. I'm the school swimming captain and also play hockey in the 2nd XI. Both of these are great – I have a chance to play around with my friends and keep up my fitness!

Music is another key element in my life. I play the alto sax, and although I have achieved grade five, I prefer to play in groups, and am a member of several bands at school. When I'm not doing any of these things, I quite enjoy the cinema and chilling out with friends – playing computer games, watching football, etc.

How much is the business turning over now and what are your plans for it?

Well, we haven't completed this year's accounts yet, but I think we will have sold about £20,000 of footwear – not too bad for our first year! I'm not too sure where the business will go really. I have sold my stake to my brother Thomas (15), who is now running it with my mother, to allow me to concentrate on my university application to

Oxford. I think Thomas has plans to eventually sell more socks and maybe large clothing, but that is several years away.

OLIVER'S TOP TIPS

★ Don't be scared to pursue an idea. It's better to try and fail than not to try at all.

★ Try and keep everything local. If you can, finance it yourself or through the family. That way, if you mess it up, you won't have the bank manager banging on your front door; the worst that will happen is that Mum will refuse to cook you dinner for a few days! Also try to *do* things yourself rather than subcontracting it out to other companies who will charge a lot.

★ Keep it in perspective. Even if you don't make a lot of money, the experience will have been priceless. This is certainly true in my case. Remember to maintain ambitious, but realistic, goals.

OK, so what might *your* idea be? There are lots of different ways to look at ideas. Try the following.

Looking at something differently: Some history books say famous American inventor Thomas Edison created the lightbulb. In fact he built on other people's work with electric lamps to make a better device, the modern lightbulb, that was more practical than the previous types.

Putting someone else's invention to work: Dominic McVey was the bloke who started the craze for mini-scooters when he spotted them on the Internet. He bought the European distribution rights and made £7 million flogging them.

Doing something interesting with something seemingly boring: You wouldn't have thought flooring was the way to riches. Dawn Gibbins would disagree. By creating new types of flooring, her Flowcrete business is worth an estimated £25 million.

Having an idea that doesn't have to be obviously commercial: Think of Marie Curie, who discovered radioactive metals, or Tim Berners Lee, the man who helped create the World Wide Web.

Transforming an old industry: Ikea boss Ingvar Kamprad saw that people wanted cheap furniture that was stylish. In this way his company changed the rules of selling and revolutionized shopping for the home.

Doing something fun: Charles Darrow became the first 'game' millionaire when he sold the rights to his invention – Monopoly.

BANK ON THIS
Here's a Bit of Ideas-ology

Stick to what you know: The best business ideas are usually right under your nose.

Get out more: Although it doesn't hurt if your nose goes walkabout. Sitting pondering in your bedroom could get a bit boring, but work experience, hobbies and interests, sports, socializing and exploring will all widen your knowledge and experience.

Work out what doesn't work: Could anything be done better?

And study what does: Become a fan of great ideas and inventions. Analyse what makes them so fab. Are they simple? Cheap? Easy to operate? Fun?

Be an explorer: The market's currently full of new horizons and that means barrel-loads of opportunities for new ideas. Work your way round the Internet, Google, MySpace, iPods. What's still waiting to be invented?

Here's someone who made millions out of an object that had been invented years before and which everyone else considered pretty humdrum . . .

HOT SEAT:
JAMES DYSON

Fast facts

Who: *The man who swept the board with a revolutionary vacuum cleaner.*

Success factor: *Became a billionaire after inventing the dual-cyclone, bagless cleaner. His firm, Dyson, employs 1,600 people worldwide.*

Trivia bite: *He also invented the Ballbarrow, a wheelbarrow with a ball instead of a wheel to make it more manoeuvrable.*

Was there a moment when you decided to invent things? What was your first invention?

I'm not sure I had one moment when I decided that I wanted to be an inventor or a designer. This is probably because I didn't get the chance to make anything when I was at school. Unfortunately, there wasn't a subject as inspiring as Design and Technology when I was at school. The best opportunity I had was making wonky matchstick holders in woodwork. Consequently, I got into invention quite late in the day, when I was studying furniture design at the Royal College of Art. My first real achievement was the Sea Truck, a high-speed boat with a flat hull, which I designed and put into production while working in my final year in an engineering company called Rotork, based in Bath.

How did you get inspired and how would you advise teenagers to do the same?

Everything that I've ever designed has been based on my own frustrations. The idea for the first dual-cyclone vacuum cleaner was born out of my bemusement and anger at finding that after vacuuming just one room of my house, the bag on my Hoover had clogged, and the suction had failed. I set out to make something better, as the fundamental design for the vacuum cleaner hadn't been altered for almost a century. If you ever get annoyed with your rucksack, iPod or electric toothbrush, then I'd advise you to think about how it could be made better. You might just come up with something that could improve people's lives.

Did you find that school helped or hindered you?

I think education is very important, and being at school taught me a lot of very useful lessons that weren't always taught in the classroom. It taught me how to monopolize on my strengths. What it didn't teach me was anything useful about designing or engineering. In fact, I'm sure I've surprised a few of my teachers in turning out like

I did. I'm sure that if I had had the chance to do D&T at school, I would have discovered my passion for designing and engineering earlier on.

Do you think that starting young has any particular benefits in business?

Yes, I do. To make a success of yourself in any kind of industry, but especially in engineering, you have to be sure of yourself and your invention or design. The sooner you start meddling in the real world of engineering, the quicker you'll build up your self-confidence, which will enable you to stick to your guns, even when people ridicule your ideas.

How would you advise young people to finance their ideas?

In my business – engineering – it's essential to protect your idea if you're to have a chance at making money. So understanding the intellectual property system is key. The Patent Office's website (*www.patent.gov.uk*) has lots of useful information on what to do.

What was your biggest setback and how did you deal with it?

I've had a lot of setbacks in my career, and have dealt with them by grim determination and believing in myself. When trying to convince people to back my invention the phrase I heard at every turn was 'But, James, if there were a better kind of vacuum cleaner, Hoover or Electrolux would have already made it'. People laughed, and I went into a lot of debt and occasional depression, but had the guts to keep believing in myself.

What luxury do you spoil yourself with now you have 'made it'?

I don't really think of myself as having 'made it'. I've built some vacuum cleaners and a successful business, but what continues to inspire me is the chance to keep improving things, so I don't think I'll ever give up my day job!

Are there any areas you think young people should target?
I think that we need young creative minds in all areas of business and industry. However, the area closest to my heart is, of course, design and engineering. Britain needs many more engineering graduates to fill the 37,000 job vacancies that come up annually. The industry is suffering from lack of talent and lack of resources. I believe that Britain is a nation of very creative individuals, and I want young people to go into engineering to experience the challenge and satisfaction that it can bring.

What would you say is the secret of your success and what is the biggest risk for young people starting out?
I think I simply had a good idea and never gave up on it. I'm actually worried that young people are not exposed to enough risks during their education. Although young people should be encouraged, I think they also need to experience failure as a way of learning how to improve. In this way, you learn not to give up.

What is the best thing about being famous and can you have too much too soon?
Being 'famous' is not something that I like to be known for. Rather than being famous for fame's sake, I'm thankful that my name is associated with something that I have created. It worries me that more and more school children are growing up with aspirations of 'being famous' rather than creating or achieving something worthy of fame. I continue to be involved in all the design work at Dyson, and so I'm honestly not bothered if people think of me as 'famous'. I'm just doing my job, and what I've always loved doing.

Where do you do your best thinking?

Engineering is a career that's full of mixed blessings. Critical thinking is integral to the work of an engineer, and something that you learn very quickly. However, it's very difficult to take your engineer's hat off and stop analysing everything you come into contact with. So, everywhere I go, I'm continually thinking about how I could make things better. It's something that annoys my friends and family. The Eureka moments made so famous by an in-the-buff-Archimedes are actually quite rare in an inventor's life.

JAMES'S TOP TIPS

★ Think critically. Analyse the things you use every day and think about whether they do really offer the best solution.

★ When you're sure you've got a good idea, never give up on it. So much potential can be lost when people fall at the first hurdle.

★ Don't be afraid to be different. That's how change happens and things get better.

Growing Your Big Idea

Once you've got something in mind, it's time to take it through some vigorous checks.

Check 1: Never cling on to a business idea out of pride. An idea is an idea – there are plenty of others out there. Although it's good to have vision and energy, if an idea starts to stink it's best put down. Don't hang on in there just for the hell of it.

Check 2: Run it past a cross-section of friends and family – people you trust. Go out there and talk to potential customers. Find out if it's something they're interested in. If you have to start persuading them, it's probably not such a good idea after all.

Check 3: Look at the competition. Who else is offering the same as you?

Check 4: Do research on the Internet. Search for rival companies and names. Visit university library sites for free info. See how much products sell for on eBay and how many people want to buy.

Here's a bright young entrepreneur who had a brilliant engineering idea and turned it into a commercial project.

HOT SEAT:
TANYA BUDD

Fast facts
Who: At 17 she invented Hypo Hoist, a device for getting unconscious people out of water.
Success factor: Experts reckon her revolutionary idea could transform safety at sea. Tanya has already sold more than 3,000 of the £300 products.
Trivia bite: When she won a Young Engineer for Britain Award she admits that she didn't even know what engineering was.

What was the first thing you ever invented?
My first significant invention was a fold-away, wall-mounted table and chair unit without legs! I designed and manufactured this for my A level Product Design-resistant Materials course, which I got a grade A for.

How did you get the idea for Hypo Hoist?
I would like to say the success of Hypo Hoist was all hard work, but my Eureka moment came when messing around on the water on a summer's afternoon! We were practising sailing back to someone who had fallen over the side when I discovered how difficult it is to

get a heavy waterlogged person back on to a yacht. I realized that it is impossible to recover a casualty by yourself, especially if they are unconscious. A definite design problem!

I suppose most people would have stopped there, but I didn't. I asked myself whether there might be significant market potential for such a product and if yes, whether it was worth spending some time and money on coming up with a solution to the problem.

In some respects, coming up with the solution was the easy bit, getting the Hypo Hoist into production was a real learning experience.

What's the biggest challenge you faced?

One of the most challenging tasks was taking this idea and actually developing it into a working prototype. You need to compose an in-depth design specification and stick to it like glue, so that your final design will be a success. You need to design the product not just for use but also for misuse and abuse, taking into the equation both manufacture and assembly processes.

The largest challenge of all is getting your product to market. There are many fantastic products out there that don't make it, but that doesn't mean yours won't. Patent your product, and trademark the name so that you, the designer and the product, get recognized as one. Then get in the public's view – enter competitions, go to design and engineering events and get noticed, and network. The contacts you will gain will be amazing and you never know when you may need them. This will also help you with finding a partner company, someone who will take your product into production. Organize meetings with several and choose the business you feel comfortable working with. I can guarantee that the experience you will gain will be invaluable to your future.

Engineering is still something of a male-dominated world. Why do you think that is and what can be done about it?

Engineering is a vital part of all our lives and underpins virtually everything we come into contact with, but far too many young people who would find engineering a fascinating and rewarding career are put off by engineering's portrayal as dull, dirty and unexciting. Engineers are shaping the future and will be involved in resolving the big issues of today, such as sustainability, energy supply, transport and climate change. To me, and I believe a lot of other young people, that really is exciting and it is something that I would like to be involved in.

Before my involvement with Young Engineers I had not considered a career in engineering. I was told about every other possible career. It was suggested to me that I would enjoy doing a degree in biology, chemistry or medicine. Engineering, however, was never discussed. I asked myself, 'Was this because I am a girl?' But it wasn't! I realized that teachers and careers advisers mainly tend to talk about and encourage students to do things that they are knowledgeable about and have experience of. I had teachers who were chemists and biologists, who had children in medicine, but there were no engineers! Now this, I believe, was the issue. In most schools there are very few, if any, graduate engineers and engineering is not taught as a subject very widely, which needs to change!

The possibilities for young engineers are endless, and this is the reason why I am now studying Engineering at Brunel University.

However, engineers don't just design products, they have to be able to market their products or components, be good communicators, have a firm grasp on financial controls, costs and profitability. Like everything, engineering is about business and success. It is about being truly enterprising.

Where do you do your best thinking?
In bed, believe it or not! I work so hard during the day on both my business and coursework I don't get the time to have free thinking space. My mind is so buzzing when I try to go to sleep that I normally jump out of bed with my ideas!

What is the ultimate invention you'd like to make?

Oh, there are many engineering feats that I would have loved to have taken part in, but who knows what the future holds with new and improving technologies and materials, and I haven't thought of my ultimate invention yet!

What engineering feat do you most admire?

I personally think the Concorde was one of many outstanding feats of British engineering and design. It's just a great shame that the aircraft was not economical enough to be sustainable, otherwise we would be living in a world of supersonic aviation transportation, where we would fly to other continents for work without a second thought, like we get on a train to London.

TANYA'S TOP TIPS

★ Think laterally. Think beyond the norm and push engineering boundaries to the limits.

★ Don't be afraid to ask questions, and always be willing to listen and learn from experts in all fields, not just engineering. To be able to harvest a broad range of knowledge and experience is priceless.

★ Philippe Jarry from Airbus said something to me at an engineering conference. His words really hit home and summed up my whole attitude to life. He said, 'Let's do it!'

Now it's time to find out how you take your idea – whatever it is – and look at how to grow it into a business. This means persuading other people that it's as good as you think it is. It's easy to stall at this point, sitting on your idea or invention and taking it no further, but you've seen how people like Tanya and James took the next steps to getting them off the ground.

It's all about making sure your idea flies rather than just gathering dust in your brain!

4.
BUILDING YOUR BIZ-ILLION

You've got your brilliant idea and you're keener than the keenest brand of mustard. You know you're the next Stelios and you're gagging to get going. What next?

This chapter is about how to get your idea off the ground using business plans, money, pitching and negotiation. Are you starting to feel like an entrepreneur yet? You will be by the end of this chapter!

MILLI-FACT
53 per cent of teenagers say they want to start their own business.

If you've ever watched *Dragons' Den* on TV you'll have seen all those budding business whizzes trying to pitch their products, from water-free egg cookers to umbrella vending machines, to a panel of business big cheeses. Peter Jones is the cool-looking one in pinstripes who decides whether to invest or eject and here are some thoughts from him on how to get your business moving.

HOT SEAT:
PETER JONES

Fast facts

Who: *The star of TV's Dragons' Den, American Inventor and Tycoon who started out in business aged 16.*

Success factor: *He set up Phones International, has his own TV company and is personally worth £180 million according to The Sunday Times Rich List. And he did it all before he was 40.*

Trivia bite: *Peter used to live on an estate in Surrey, which features the 100-acre wood made famous in Winnie the Pooh.*

When did you start coming up with business ideas?

I used to dream about setting up a business when I was sitting in my father's office chair. I wasn't sure how I was going to do it, but I knew that I wanted to be in charge of a large, successful corporation. I was 7 at the time and I pretended to send telexes (which was the way messages were sent – the fax machine replaced the telex) and issue instructions to people.

How did you set up your first venture? Was there a moment of inspiration?

I always loved playing tennis, and I began by helping one of the older coaches to teach the other children. From this I learnt many valuable skills, and I explored many aspects of coaching. This gave me brilliant insight, but setting up by myself was not easy. I needed to acquire an official qualification to prove my worth to my customers, and to gain the same skills as my mentor. On top of this, I had to do my own marketing, mailing to all of the parents, offering weekend sessions based upon skill level. It involved me handling my own finance, but I learnt a lot working for someone who did it previously. Because of previous experience I was able to create a successful academy and introduce ideas to make it exciting. It became very popular.

As a young person, what attitude did you have to have to get where you are? Did school help or hinder you?

I always had a very positive can-do attitude towards my activities. I pursued my dreams. I was not the most studious pupil. I think I was keener on establishing my independence and forging my own path than conforming to an academic existence. Sport and economics were my favourite pastimes.

Did you ever find your young age meant you weren't taken seriously?

I was lucky: being tall people often mistook me for being older than I was. It is a problem, but again, for the job that I was doing – tennis coaching – my skills were more important than my age. In fact, my youth was probably helpful in supporting my sporting image. I do get many letters from young people posing this question, and it is clearly an issue. I think that as long as you are honest, support any claims that you make and deliver the services you promise, then you gain respect. Word of mouth is one of the most effective ways of marketing a business. After my tennis academy, I started a computer business when I was 17 and in my early twenties had to conduct many business meetings, often with people twice my age. I really enjoyed this challenge.

How would you suggest young people finance their ideas?

You don't need a huge amount of start-up capital to begin a business. Sell whatever you can – books, games, toys – and reinvest the money that you make. Keep reinvesting any money you make. Remember, in business cash is king, so invest and spend it wisely. Never lose sight of your idea, but do not be afraid to alter and develop it as you learn.

What was your biggest setback and how did you deal with it?

I lost all of my wealth in my twenties because I was not careful enough. It was a setback, but one of my mottoes is 'There is no such thing as failure, only feedback'. From this struggle, I learnt to be more meticulous with my businesses, and ensure that I covered all my bases. I joined a corporate firm, gaining experience and making contacts, until I had enough capital to branch out on my own again. I made sure I did not make the same mistakes again.

What luxury do you spoil yourself with?

I love cars and I think they are my biggest weakness.

You've done well in the communications industry. Which area do you think young people should target and why?

I think that entrepreneurs should become involved in what they are passionate about. Only by being passionate about what you are doing will you be prepared to go that extra mile. I only ever invest in things that I really believe in. After all, if you are going to spend all of your time on something, you have to enjoy it.

What is the secret of your success and what is the biggest risk for young people starting out?

My success comes from my personal drive and a constant willingness to learn and absorb new skills. I think the biggest risk that youngsters face is a lack of experience and a lack of places to turn to find this knowledge. I really believe there should be an effective business syllabus taught in schools, a syllabus that is formed by entrepreneurs and business people who have experienced the problems that businesses face, rather than by academics. Don't be afraid to ask advice and opinions from everyone around you – learn from the experience of others.

What is the best thing about being famous and can you have too much too soon?

The best thing about being famous is that it opens doors to people that I would not normally get the chance to meet. I live a very normal existence and I have a great set of friends around me, who I have known since childhood. I don't think it ever does go to my head. Having lost all my wealth in my twenties, I am aware of the pitfalls of success. Anyway, it might be short-lived, so I will enjoy it while it lasts!

Where do you do your best thinking?

I'm always thinking. I relax by coming up with new business propositions! Although I find my best ideas come when I sound them out by talking to others. Ideas develop when they are considered from many different perspectives and so discussing them helps. I often advise people to pitch their business ideas to others, to friends and family even, to listen to their opinions.

You are known as a bit of a snappy dresser. What clothes should budding entrepreneurs wear?

My advice on dress code is to always wear what is appropriate for the environment that you work in. It is important to make people feel comfortable around you. If you are in a corporate environment, you should wear a smart suit, as this is the acceptable dress code. If you are working in a media environment, for example, you can wear more casual clothes. When I started my production company, PJTV, I felt very out of place in my suit among the more casual members of my team. In contrast, some of my businesses have a very strict dress code in place. You must be able to adapt to the situation that you are in. Above all else though, whatever you wear, it is important to be well groomed and clean. When you feel good, it comes across to people you interact with.

PETER'S TOP TIPS

★ Research and test your idea thoroughly.
★ Formulate a concise business outline.
★ Never give up.

Pitch your business idea direct to Peter at *www.peterjones.tv*

So, as Peter says, you don't need a huge amount of cash to start your business. But you have to be adaptable and be prepared to learn some business essentials before you can get your idea off the ground. And what does he mean by a business outline? He means that first you'll need a cunning plan! A business plan, that is.

Why a Business Plan?

Ideas are great. But they don't make money on their own. To make money from your great idea you're going to have to turn it from an idea in your head or on paper into something real. This means writing a business plan.

First, put on paper all the facts, figures and forecasts connected with your idea.

Then, list all your skills plus the enthusiasm, confidence and sense of vision and purpose that you possess in bucketloads.

MILLI-MOUTH

❝When I started out in business, I spent a great deal of time researching every detail that might be pertinent to the deal I was interested in making. I still do the same today. People often comment on how quickly I operate, but the reason I can move quickly is that I've done the background work first, which no one usually sees. I prepare myself thoroughly, and then when it is time to move ahead, I am ready to sprint.❞ – *Donald Trump, from the US version of* The Apprentice

How Your Plan Comes Together

A good business plan should have the following headings:

1. Your idea: Present it as a vision. Use your passion while thinking about these questions. Why is it such a good idea? What makes it different? Where is the gap in the market? Who's gagging to buy it?

2. Timing: What's going on in the world to make your idea right for now?

3. What success looks like: Where is this idea going? How will it grow? Nationwide chain of stores? Global? Exclusive? How many customers will it get? What sort of turnover will it pull in? How will you measure its success?

4. Staff: Who's involved in your idea so far? What do they do? How do *you* get involved? What makes you special?

5. Sales: How or where can your idea be sold?

6. Competition: What's already out there? What's to stop anyone else running with your idea? Why is it so special? Can it be copied or lifted? (Remember that a great idea is only worth money if no one else can nick it.)

7. Money: How much do you need to get going? Where do you think it might come from? (Robbing a bank is never an impressive option.)

8. Next steps: Does your idea have a natural lifespan? Where would your business go if it begins to run out of steam? Great to do Ear-Wigs but they are seasonal and open to fashion whims. Are there future plans for spin-offs if that happens? Ear-Wigs for pets? Finger-Wigs? False eyelashes?)

BANK ON THIS

*Some Key Words and Facts to Put into
Your Business Plan*

'Profit margin' The difference between how much your product will sell for and the costs to make or prepare it.

'Overheads' The money you'll pay out to run your business. Most of these exist even if you're not selling anything.

'Variable costs' These are things you only have to buy or spend money on if you're making or selling something, like the materials you need to make your product.

'Cash flow' How long will it take to get your money from your customers? Many businesses go bust because they haven't got the money to pay their suppliers. The businesses may be owed a lot, but they can't pay their debts until they receive it. This creates what's known as a 'cash-flow problem'.

'Tax and VAT' Did you forget it? Surely not! These are sums of money that get taken out of your profit by the government to pay for things like the NHS. Read more about it at *www.hmrc.gov.uk*

'Marketing costs' Very few ideas or products sell well from the word go. How are you going to let people know your service/products are available? Will you need to advertise? Create a website? Give out fliers?

Get publicity? Do your homework and find out how much this might cost. 'Viral marketing' means getting your product known via word of mouth. It's a very effective sales tool, especially for the youth market, and it's also very cheap. However it's difficult to manage and very unreliable.

'Interest on loans' If you're old enough to borrow money, the sad fact is that it's not a gift, you're going to have to pay it back. Boo!

'Services' If all this talk of money makes your head spin, you might need to hire an accountant pronto. Find out how much he/she would charge.

Sound daunting? It needn't be. Here's a guy who kicked off his first business at the tender age of 10.

HOT SEAT:
BEN WAY

Fast facts

Who: *Whizz-kid who was setting up multi-million-pound deals before he was 19.*

Success factor: *Set up his first company, aged 15, from his bedroom, then hit the big time with an Internet search tool called Waysearch. He was New Business Millennium Young Entrepreneur of the Year in 2000 and now runs a company called Rainmakers, which develops new technologies.*

Trivia bite: *Starred in Channel 4's Secret Millionaire, where he went undercover to give away £40,000 to good causes.*

How to be a Teenage Millionaire

Did you always want to be a millionaire?
No, being a millionaire wasn't my aim when I was young. I knew I was different, and wanted to run my own thing. The money was more of a by-product of success, rather than being my goal.

What was your first-ever business idea?
'Megaswap' was my first idea, where I charged a small fee to act as an agent, arranging swaps of cartridge computer games. I was 10 at the time!

What was the hardest thing about trying to achieve success in business as a teenager?
Being young in business is a double-edged sword. On the one hand, people are impressed with someone so young being a competent businessman. On the other, people don't take you so seriously. It's also hard on a transactional basis – routine operations become very difficult; for example, obtaining a business bank account or arranging legal documents.

Did your dyslexia hold you back?
That was never really a problem. My dyslexia causes me problems with remembering people's names, and who I've met before, and that was difficult when meeting with businessmen. But being dyslexic didn't affect my business skills or how I was treated – it wasn't really an issue.

How did you get business people to invest £25 million in you?
Some investors saw me on a TV programme, called me and said they were looking to spend some money and did I have any good ideas. Of course I said yes. I didn't know how much to ask for, but thought £25 million sounded like a good number. Fortunately, they responded by saying that's exactly the amount they were looking to

invest! During the negotiations, I changed the office I had in my house to a boardroom, and drew up business plans. I had to consider who I was dealing with, and I knew that was what would get me taken seriously.

What kinds of business do you think teenagers should look at and why?
Electronic commerce is one of the largest-growing areas, so it's the logical place to start. Be entrepreneurial – get involved in all sorts of things that interest you. You don't have to start your own business – trade on eBay!

When you have a million in the bank, how does that feel?
It gives you peace of mind – you don't have to worry about bills, etc. It's great not having to rely on others to support you. *But* it doesn't stop you from striving onwards – there's always more to gain!

What luxuries do you spoil yourself with?
Buying a home was my biggest luxury. I spend a lot on home improvements. I also like going on holidays – my last was to the Seychelles. Of course I love having the latest gadgets, although it's not essential, just fun.

You lost money as well as made it. How did you pick yourself up?
The support of friends was a huge help to me. Also I put in a lot of hard work to bring myself back. To anyone in this situation, I would say believe in yourself and learn from your mistakes.

What are the dangers of making a lot of money young and how would you advise teens to cope with it?
It's easy to grow up too quickly, to lose your innocence. Keep good friends around you, and don't let it go to your head!

You've been on TV 'giving something back'. Why is this important?

At the time in my life when I lost everything, someone was kind enough to take me under his wing and look after me. I have been inspired to do the same for other people. I want to be there for others, as someone was there for me.

Which famous person that you have met were you in awe of?

Simon Woodroffe, founder of YO! Sushi, who I am now friends with. He is one of the few people who says exactly what he thinks, and doesn't necessarily do what is expected of him just to please others!

BEN'S TOP TIPS

★ Believe in yourself.

★ If you fail, keep trying. Don't give up.

★ Don't try to take huge leaps, just keep making small steps, and that steady progress will get you there.

★ Don't try to do everything – know what you're good at and what you're not. Work hard at what you can do well, and let others get on with the rest!

MILLI-FACT

After six years, 80 per cent of business start-ups aren't trading any more.

MILLI-MOUTH

'Success is going from failure to failure without a loss of enthusiasm.' – *Prime Minister Winston Churchill*

Now you'll need to decide what sort of business you'd like to be. This doesn't matter if you're only planning to make a few bob washing your mate's mum's car. However, if you're going to be washing 100 cars, then it's become a business

---

BANK ON THIS

What Outfit Suits Me?

There are three ways to trade:

Sole trader: This means working on your own, like a window cleaner or a freelance fitness trainer. There's little paperwork and even less protection: you will be liable for your debts. You'll need to register as self-employed with the Inland Revenue (*www.hmrc.gov.uk*). If you start to expand you might need to set up a partnership or a limited company.

Partnership: You may decide to work with someone else, possibly a friend or relative. You share the risk and the profits, as well as the fun of running a company with a like-minded person. Don't make the arrangements too casually. Draw up an agreement between you both so that things don't get sticky if it goes wrong. A solicitor may cost money but it could avoid problems in the future. What if one of you wants to pull out or your partner thinks you aren't working hard enough? Remember to make it a formal partnership as soon as possible.

Limited company: This is a company with 'Ltd' after its name. Investors and customers may take you more

---

seriously if you are a limited company. 'Limited' means you don't lose everything if your business goes bust. There are tax issues and lots of paperwork. You must register as a company with Companies House at *www.companieshouse.gov.uk*

Once you've decided on your business type, you need to start thinking about . . .

Scaling Up

Sounds like something to do with scraping the skin off a fish? In fact, scaling up is just business jargon for making sure you've got an idea that can grow, often to the point where the sky's the limit. Scaling up means the difference between starting a business that becomes your job and starting a business that you can sell or expand. Scalability is vital if you want to be a business entrepreneur but not so important if you're happy to keep your business very small.

You don't have to scale up, but it's good to know your options before you start out. There's no such thing as early days when you're planning to make a mint. Here's a tip as you scratch your head and meditate in the loo trying to come up with your stonking great idea: work out if it's a business that can be scaled up or not.

Let's take our Ear-Wigs. If you're the only one making them, as orders increase you're going to get busy – maybe very busy. There will be puffs of smoke coming out of your sewing machine and you'll be seeing a lot less of your mates. There will be a lid on income from this business as it'll depend on how many Ear-Wigs you can find the time and energy to make.

However, let's say your Ear-Wigs can be manufactured elsewhere. As the orders come in you just farm out the work, because costed into your Ear-Wigs is money to pay other people to make them for you. Then, when the trend catches on big time, you can either franchise the business (allow other people to buy the idea and make their own Ear-Wigs in Scunthorpe or Stockholm) or you could sell it and start another even better business.

When you look at your brilliant idea, check how far it's scalable. Then see if that fits in with your plans and dreams. If it's something only you can do yourself, it will put a limit on your profits, so that island in the sun might just have to stay a dream. If you really want the millionaire lifestyle, though, you might need to go back to the drawing board and come up with an idea that can be scaled up instead.

MILLI-FACT

The world's oldest business is reckoned to be a Japanese hotel called Hoshi Ryokan, founded in 718 and still going!

BANK ON THIS

Five Vital Tips About Turning Your Idea into a Business

★ **Know your product:** Know how it works and be able to demonstrate it easily.

★ **Know your profit margin:** The gap between the selling price and the manufacturing costs.

★ **Know your customer:** Who'll want it and how much will they pay to get it?

★ **Know why they'll want to buy it from you:** rather than from a competitor.

★ **Know that the idea is scalable.**

Simon Woodroffe's restaurant idea spread like a forest fire, without any need for him to wait tables or scrub dirty plates in the kitchen.

HOT SEAT:
SIMON WOODROFFE

Fast facts
Who: *Founder of the YO! Sushi restaurant chain that has branches all over the world.*
Success factor: *Realized that food delivered on conveyor belts could be cool. He eventually sold a portion of his shares for £10 million. He was on the first series of Dragons' Den.*
Trivia bite: *Left school with just two O levels (the old name for GCSEs).*

You were once quoted as saying it's not difficult to make a million pounds. Is the same true for a teenager?

When you're young you tend to think less that things will be difficult. You also have fewer worries about things going wrong and that can be a help. Experience or lack of it can work both ways – good or bad.

What were you like at school?

I wasn't very academic. I left with two O levels in French and maths, so I always had to earn a living. I didn't really pay attention in class. I was the original 'Could try harder'! In many ways I never believed I could do it. I wasn't very good in terms of behaviour but I wasn't terrible either.

What inspired you as a young person?

I was inspired by a visit to the Aston Martin factory when I was 11. We saw the James Bond car. I became interested in design and building things. I think schools should work hard to create a passion and interest in how the world works.

What do you see as good business opportunities for teens?
My daughter's 17 and she's set up Smooch, a business organizing parties for under-age teenagers at glamorous venues. The first is being held at the Embassy club in aid of the Teenage Cancer Trust. The NFTE [National Foundation for Teaching Entrepreneurship] charity has seen teenagers run businesses, doing everything from repairing model racing cars, making T-shirts and buying from cash and carries to sell on at school to selling reading glasses direct via the Internet. Teenagers have less fear and are less likely to say 'I can't do that'. They also tend to put their money back into building their businesses rather than spending it on things like drugs or alcohol. Building the business becomes their drug.

Didn't you start out late, at about 40?
I did! I was making and selling belts at the age of 17, then I was a roadie . . . I had a design business, I sold TV rights . . .

So at what point did you think 'I've made it'?
Probably when I sold part of YO! Sushi three years ago.

What is the best thing about being a millionaire?
Freedom from financial anxiety.

And the worst thing?
There's nothing bad I can think of. You can get het up a bit, that's all.

How do you dress like a millionaire?
I never wear black shoes or brown shoes and I think if you wear grey shoes you've got something wrong with you! It's good to find your own idiosyncrasy. I bought a pair of lime green shoes once

from Harvey Nicholls for about £50. When I wore them I saw two attractive women looking at them then looking up at me and smiling. I now own a pair of shoes in yellow, a pair in red . . . blue . . . green . . . salmon . . . purple, all handmade in suede.

Do millionaires do funny?
I'm very good at telling jokes.

MILLI-FACT
Not all millionaire occupations are glamorous. In the US three of the top-rated businesses are dredging, mushroom-growing and pest control.

No Fun Without Funds

While you might not need much money to start your business, you're going to need some to help it take off. To convince someone else to stump up some cash you'll need to 'pitch'. This means talking about your business in a way that will convince others to join in and invest.

Pitching might sound daunting, but as long as you've got passion in your own idea and you've done your homework (that business plan), it can be fun. Pitching is a two-way process: you listen as much (or maybe even more) than you speak. Even if your pitch doesn't work with one person, the reasons they give could help your next pitch.

Here are some ideas of where you might find finance.

Parents or Relatives
This is the easy option for an easy touch, which could be exactly why you shouldn't borrow from them. Will they be as critical or

knowledgeable as a professional? And how ghastly if you lose all their money. There are many reasons why this can be a good option but it can also put pressure on family relationships.

If your parents are loaded to the point that they really won't notice a loss, you could try your luck. However, if you're taking their entire savings and losing it will cost them dear, then lay off.

Angels and Venture Capitalists

These are people who invest in new businesses or ideas, usually for a share of the business. Some will even add their weight and experience to growing the business or getting it off the ground. Business-support agencies often have networking facilities that can help introduce you to the right angel.

Banks

They give out loans all the time, but they usually want some sort of security against it, like a house. Your age could be a barrier here.

Grants

The government have all sorts of grants available to start up businesses. See *www.businesslink.gov.uk* for details. Support organizations also give out some grants.

Special Schemes

Special schemes operate in some schools to help get a taste of what it's like to start a business. For example, the Make Your Mark With A Tenner scheme, funded by the founder of the Entrepreneur Channel, has allowed young people to show what they could do – when given £10. One group pooled their tenners, made a CD and sold it for a profit. See *www.starttalkingideas.org* for more information.

BANK ON THIS

Get a NESTA Egg

Their name, National Endowment for Science, Technology and the Arts, may be a bit of a mouthful. But give them a shout and they might invest in your innovative business idea. NESTA is all about identifying start-up companies with great ideas and helping them to get going with a bit of funding. They provide people with knowledge to support small start-ups in everything from healthcare to engineering.

See *www.nesta.org.uk*

MILLI-FACT

Don't get the blues – painting your office this colour has been proven to lower motivation.

Skills and Thrills

Your next step is to learn the three biggest skills of pitching: how to do meetings, how to present and how to negotiate. The great news is that all three are fun, and the even greater news is that they're hugely useful whatever you chose to do with your life.

If you find speaking to strangers daunting, it's probably just lack of experience, so read your way through these simple tips and then get out there and try out your talents for size!

How to do Meetings

Your pitch could involve a meeting. This will probably be at the other person's office, although telephone conferencing is a popular option as it means chatting over the phone rather than travelling.

Meetings mean just that – a chance to meet other people and talk through your ideas. Your meeting could be with one person or a group. The format might be similar to a job interview with you on one side of a desk and a panel on the other, or it could be much more casual, with settees and a coffee table instead. Some meetings even take place in restaurants or canteens.

You could be asked to do a formal presentation, in which read on for hot tips to make sure yours goes well. Or it might be chat and questions.

A meeting with a client or finance bod is your chance to shine and sell. However it can also be a grade A opportunity to make a prize prat of yourself. Here are ten tips to make sure your meetings go to plan:

★ Turn up on time. Better still, be early. Being late shows lack of respect for the person you're seeing. Time is expensive in business and wasting someone else's can cause trouble. Excuses don't help. Nobody likes to wait for someone to crawl out of bed and on to a bus.

★ Never go looking like a scruff-bag. Polish your shoes and maybe get that suit out.

★ Spend time planning what you want to happen as a result of the meeting and how you can make that happen.

★ Give good shake. Let the other person offer their hand first, but return it with confidence. And if there are several people, shake your way round the group.

★ You might find the meeting scary, but make sure you say something within the first three minutes. The longer you sit in silence, the harder it'll be to get going. And when you do, you'll get one of those Kermit-sized frogs in your throat and start coughing. By speaking up quickly you'll break the ice and then your confidence will grow and you'll start to relax.

★ Listen, don't interrupt.

★ Switch off your mobile.

★ Make sure you've got all your facts with you and then some. Take more facts and figures than you think you'll need, just in case.

★ Take paper copies as handouts. Think of what they'll want to know and find out all the answers. Pitching up with a nice smile and bags of enthusiasm isn't enough. They'll want to know you've done your homework too.

★ Plan for a no as well as for a yes. It's good to be focused on a positive result, but it also helps to plan what you'll do if you get turned down. It's vital to remember that it's not a fail if you do, just a temporary setback. If they do turn your idea down, don't act like you're on the *X Factor* and fling water over them, cry or get your nan in to tell them off. Think onwards and upwards instead. These people might be telling you to tweak your idea and come back again, or they could be impressed with you even if your idea's not for them. Remember to smile, thank them and ask for their advice for the future.

How to Present Your Idea

Pitching your idea might mean making a presentation. This is where you stand (or sit) in front of a group of people and tell them all about your ideas and plans.

Dragons' Den makes presenting look like a painful business, but it doesn't have to be. Seeing all those wannabe tycoons squirm as they pitch to a row of serious faces might make you feel glad you're tucked up in the comfort of your own living room . . . But pitches like that are going on all the time and you'll sell your idea or product by learning three simple steps that make the art of business presenting a bit of a doddle.

BRAIN BOX

Planning

★ Start by knowing your goal. What do you want to happen after your pitch?

★ Plan your key points around that goal. You might not have long to speak and you'll want to make all your points count. Write your key goal on a piece of paper, then make sure your key points all hang off that goal. Less is more, so cut the waffle.

★ Structure your talk. When you make notes put all your ideas under five headings: S P L O T. S stands for subject matter, which is your product or idea. P is the point of your talk. What are your aims? L will be your limits. How long have you got to speak? How much will your listeners already know about your product? What words or terms might baffle them? O is for objections. What might they disagree with? T is for your talk. What do you need to tell them to convince them?

★ Plan your visual aids – the things you use to show them more about your product. You could be extra-professional and take a slide-show presentation, but you could also just bring samples of your idea along. Photos or diagrams are a good idea but only if they help illustrate what you're talking about.

Pitching

★ Show enthusiasm. Even if you feel nervous your keenness will be catching.

★ Empathize. This means thinking of their values as well as your own. People don't buy because it's good for the seller, they buy because it's good for them and their customers. Avoid telling them that they should buy/invest because 'It's something I've always wanted to do/It's my dream/I like a challenge/I love doing this. *Do* tell them that it's a good investment that will make them money, enhance their business or please their customers.

★ When you make a statement, back it up with facts. 'I think this product will sell in its thousands' works best when you prove it with research.

★ Try your pitch out on a friend first. See if they can think of any questions and then research the answers.

Performance

★ You don't need to be able to act or even be word-perfect to be a good presenter, just impress them with your personality and your dedication, energy and enthusiasm.

★ Notes will help you feel confident and make you stick to your points. Write presentation notes as a prompt, but don't write a script as it'll sound too formal. Speak from the heart.

★ Your body language can be more important than your words! Rehearse to make sure you feel comfortable when you get there. If you practise your body language enough you'll go into automatic-pilot mode when you get there, standing or sitting in a good position without even thinking about it. Stand in front of a full-length mirror at home to practise your start-off position. Feet should be straight and spaced apart and your hands should be loosely held in front of you.

★ Overcome any nerves by taking a moment before you start your presentation. A small but vital pause helps you check your breathing as well as focusing on your introduction.

★ Smile when you walk in. This does more than show you're friendly. Smiling will relax your facial muscles and it should get a response from them too. Once you're all smiling you'll be feeling empathy as it's the quickest way to create rapport with strangers.

★ There's no need to complicate things just to impress. Keep your talk simple, with a few strong points.

★ Feel free to use your hands when you talk. Using hand gestures means people listen 30 per cent more to what you're saying.

★ Plan for questions. Even let them interrupt you if they want to. It shows they're interested.

★ Nobody knows everything. If you don't know the answer to one of their questions it's not a problem, just offer to find out and get back to them. Try not to bluff because they'll spot you're lying and feel they can't trust you.

★ If you're pitching to a group of people, include them all with your eye contact, even the quiet ones and especially the ugly ones. If one person asks a question, answer to the whole group.

★ Have contact details ready for the end of your talk. If you can get some visiting cards done, they'll make you look thoughtful and professional. Try websites like *www.vistaprint.co.uk* for free ones.

How to Negotiate

If someone likes your pitch they might want to make you an offer. This can be your buzz moment, when you realize you've made a hit. All you need to do next is start some negotiating.

Negotiation is where you and your potential investor discuss what to do next, perhaps to agree the amount of money you need. Here are some points to keep in mind.

★ Practise. Negotiating gets easier the more you do it.

★ Always know your objectives. Otherwise it's easy to get pushed into something you don't want. There are only four possible outcomes of a negotiation and it's important to know which one you're focused on:

1. You win, they lose. Result? Well no, actually. It's usually a good thing to keep other people on your side.

2. You lose, they lose. Yes, this time nobody's happy; this is not a good result.

3. You lose, they win. Only one person goes away happy from this one – and it's not you, sadly.

4. You win, they win. Result! You emerge with a result that you both feel good about.

★ Know your bottom line – the point below or beyond which you can't go.

★ Prepare. Know your facts, like costing, profit margins, likely customers.

★ Always look for similar thinking rather than highlighting your differences.

★ Never take the negotiation personally.

★ Keep calm. Learn to ditch the emotions. If things get tricky, breathe out. Pause. Count to ten, then carry on.

★ Make sure you're negotiating with the boss. It's a waste of time discussing things with anyone other than the person who will make the final decision.

★ Listen. Always take in everything the other person has to say.

★ Keep your body language relaxed and open. Never sit with folded arms or crossed legs.

★ Be keen and firm but not pushy.

★ When you reach agreement, repeat what you've agreed. Often people hear different things.

MILLI-FACT

Lyle's Golden Syrup is Britain's oldest brand. The famous green and gold tins haven't changed their look since 1885.

Selling and Marketing Your Product

The next key stage in your product launch is marketing it. When you make your pitch you'll explain who your customers are. Now you need to work out the best way to sell to them.

Marketing is a multi-million-pound business in itself, with companies paying large sums to get their products in front of the right customers in the right way.

When you watch a programme on TV, check out the ads that pop up in the commercial break. They tell you a lot about the programme's audience because research will have been done to find out who watches the programme. Firms will decide if that's the sort of people who will buy their products. If they think they are, then they will advertise to them.

When you watch the soaps you'll find most ads are selling tea, cleaning products, furniture or snack foods because these are the things that appeal to most soap watchers. Catch a children's programme and the ads will be for toys or games. This is the point of marketing – putting yourself in the right place at the right time to catch the right sort of people. But you don't have to be a media whizz to understand the basics. Here's all you need to know at this stage in your business career about the four main ways of selling something. These are true for all businesses, big or small:

1. Networking: This means selling to people you know, who can then tell people they know. Put simply, you take your Ear-Wigs to school and your mates buy them. They, in turn, tell their mates about them and your orders increase. This word of mouth has recently got a new label: viral marketing. The Internet has made this word-of-mouth way of marketing much more important because people now have access to the entire world.

2. Retail: You borrow money and either rent your own market stall or shop or outlet. Ear-Wigs-Are-Us takes to the high street!

3. Wholesale: You sell your Ear-Wigs to another shop instead of opening your own. Less instant profit but less money needs to be laid out in the first place – and possibly there's less hassle too.

4. Online: Strutting your stuff via the World Wide Web!

Once you've decided on your customers and how you're going to sell them your product, your next step will be persuading people to buy it. This means not just putting your product in a shop but finding a way of making people want to go to that shop to buy it. Think about what makes you buy something. Take four or five products that you've bought recently. Why did you pay money for them? Was it need (as in food or toothpaste)? Because a friend had one? Did an advert persuade you to shell out? Or did you see someone you admire, like a celebrity, with it? Marketing is fascinating because it's all about basic psychology, understanding what makes people tick and how they can be influenced and persuaded.

Although marketing might seem a long way off if you're still coming up with those great ideas, it's still good to know your options for the non-too-distant future. All businesses start to involve marketing ideas in the very early stages of product design, in fact the sooner the better. In some businesses it's part of the basic design. Take record labels. Downloading and viral marketing or even sites like YouTube are currently so important in the success of a new band or record that a song might be picked for its appeal to that market. When you decide on your big idea, spend vital time thinking ahead to the marketing stages. Here are some options for plugging a product.

1. Advertising: This will nearly always cost big bucks. Think TV ads, pages in mags and billboards.

2. Celeb endorsement: If you get Kate Moss to wear your design or Jeremy Clarkson to recommend your invention or Richard and Judy to plug your book, you're away!

3. Publicity: You get your name in the papers (for all the right reasons!) or you get interviewed on TV because you're a bright young thing who can chat and entertain. And, of course, you remember to plug your product.

4. Trade shows and exhibitions: Some people hire stands at these to sell their product direct, others sell wholesale, but some just use them to get seen by the right market.

Young, Gifted and Worried?

What if you're too young to be taken seriously? What if you're asked things you don't know? What to do when the PA from hell refuses to let you speak to the boss? This next section's all about troubleshooting. Here are the answers to business problems that might keep you awake at night!

What If I'm Seen as Too Young?

★ Youth sells, so make your age one of your unique selling points (USPs). However, remember that not everyone in business might be impressed by the fact that you know all the words of the Arctic Monkeys' latest hit and can name every winner of *X Factor* and *Big Brother*. You know your age means creative thinking, energy and enthusiasm, but be prepared to persuade people who think inexperience means inept.

How Can You Impress Best When You're Talking Business?

★ However speedily you're working, try to take time to check your spelling and grammar when you're emailing potential customers.

Text-jargon won't work. Remember to always use spell-check and if you've got a mate or parent handy, get them to give things a read-through before you press 'send'. Two pairs of eyes are always better than one!

★ Don't be too informal. Emails shouldn't start with 'Hi!' and end with 'See ya!'

★ First impressions can make or break. Try to ensure that when you answer your phone or leave a voicemail you sound as professional as possible. Be careful about picking up your phone assuming it's a mate on the other end: say your full name and 'good morning/afternoon'. The same rule applies to your mobile if you're using it for business.

How Do I Sound Professional?

★ Keep a pen and paper near the phone so that callers don't have to wait for you to find them.

★ Train or bribe parents or siblings to take phone messages. Keep a pad handy for them to use and write the info you'll need on each sheet, like: name, company, phone number, email address, message, time and date. If you've got small children in the house, put the phone out of reach!

★ Remember, *always* return calls. You never really know which call's a timewaster and which one's the important one that will make everything kick off. By calling back promptly you'll show you're bright, reliable and keen.

How Do I Answer Questions?

If the idea of killer questions from a customer or business type freaks you out, you're in good company! Although it's unlikely you'll get grilled in a hostile way, it's very likely there will be questions. What if you don't know the answers?

★ Always remember that people only ask questions if they're

interested in what you do, supply or make. Think of them as a positive step.

★ Nobody knows everything and getting stuck on an answer isn't the worst thing that can happen.

★ Never make up an answer. Better to be honest and admit you don't know.

★ Sometimes it's better to create a delay. If they're asking for an on-the-spot decision you'd be wise to say you'll get back to them when you have had time to think.

★ If you don't know an answer, tell them but also offer to find out. Otherwise you'll just sound negative and uninterested.

★ You're not expected to remember shedloads of facts. Take information with you in note form, rather than in your head.

★ If you're visiting a company or potential backer get someone to give you a tough grilling first. All good businesspeople do this as it makes them prepared for anything. Ask an adult to fire killer questions at you and find out answers to any you can't handle.

How Do I Get Past a Pesky PA?

PA stands for the 'Personal Assistant' who stands between you and the people you want to do business with. Most PAs are paid to keep a huge, moat-like space between their boss and the real world. Getting across it is hard but not impossible.

★ Your youthful voice might create enough sympathy for the PA to take pity and put your call through. But don't assume that age is an advantage!

★ You might be asked what your call's about. Have a good, honest answer ready and don't start to ramble.

★ Usually you can make an appointment direct with the PA.

How Do I Look More Professional?

★ If you look too young and lightweight to knock the skin off a rice pudding, try making contact via the phone or Internet instead of face to face. Use written cues, to keep your conversation structured. Breathe out before your speak. This will slow you down if you tend to rush a bit and also drop your voice to its normal pitch.

★ Keep your speech simple. There's no need to try to talk posh or use long words. Just be normal.

★ Do good greetings. The first few seconds of contact will say lots about you. Check your appearance before entering the room.

★ Use good eye contact. By holding someone's gaze for a bit longer than normal you'll come across as confident and upbeat.

★ Smile. It's wrong to assume that all professional people wear a long face. A smile will make you look much more relaxed and open.

★ Sitting up or standing tall will make you look more confident. Sit back into the chair and either rest your hands lightly on the arms or fold them loosely in your lap.

★ Watch the barrier gestures: folded arms look unfriendly.

★ Give good shake. When you arrive at a meeting expect to shake hands. Let the host go first and let the host offer you a chair before you sit down. Keep your right hand free for handshakes. Offer a firm but friendly shake and use eye contact as you do it.

★ Use open and emphatic gestures as you speak. By using your hands you'll show confidence and energy, but don't flap them about.

★ Don't fiddle or fidget with things. Work out what to do with your hands to make you look confident and self-assured.

★ Walk energetically but without rushing. Successful people look dynamic, as though the day just isn't long enough.

★ Don't spend a lot of money on clothes. It's more important to look tidy and well-groomed.

★ Buy clothes that fit, not ones that are too tight or too trendy. Go for simple styles in darker colours

★ Stop biting your nails. It might not be easy but it's more important than you think. Most signs of nerves can be masked but those massacred cuticles could suggest anxiety.

★ Get your hair looking neat and clean.

★ Don't overdo the smellies! Too much creates the wrong sort of lasting impression. Keep it light and fresh instead.

★ Do you get sweaty under pressure? Don't worry, it's a common problem. A good deodorant will help, as will avoiding tight-fitting clothes in man-made fibres. Try the cosmetics counters too – there are products that help stop your face going shiny.

★ Blushing always feels worse than it looks. You really shouldn't worry about this one, however bad it gets. Red faces are common in business meetings and so are those annoying blotchy nerve rashes. Top professionals suffer from them too – forget about them and get on with business is the best solution.

Will I Come Across Legal Problems Because of My Age?

★ At the moment you can be a company director at any age outside Scotland and there are currently hundreds under 16. However, from October 2008 you'll only be allowed to be one under certain circumstances. Keep an eye on the latest rules and regulations by contacting Companies House, who regulate these things: *www.companieshouse.gov.uk* Your signature may not be legally binding on contracts and they can advise you on what to do.

Where Will My HQ Be?

★ If you are not going to make your home your base, then you need premises. Remember that with them comes rent and other responsibilities. Check *www.businesslink.gov.uk* for their advice.

Is There Other Stuff to Worry About?

★ Oh yes, plenty! There's tax and VAT (see *www.hmrc.gov.uk*), accounting and invoicing matters, and health and safety issues. Becoming a millionaire isn't all a bed of £50 notes, you know! The good news is, there's plenty of help and advice along the way.

How to Bounce Back

Sometimes it's hard not to be crushed by a negative experience. However there are ways to programme your thinking to make sure you make the most of every experience.

 BRAIN BOX
If It Isn't Working Out

★ Think Snakes and Ladders. When you slide down a snake you play harder to get to the next ladder.

★ Think chess. To get really good you need to lose games.

★ Think footie. When a team gets trounced they work out how to prevent it happening again.

★ Think strategy. Don't look at the trees, look at the gaps between them. If your car is heading towards a forest at 150 km/hr because your brakes have failed, you look for the gaps, not the trees. If something fails to work, look for what will work, not sob over what held you up.

★ Think babies. Ever watched a toddler learn to walk? Count how many times it lands on its bottom before it manages to stagger a few feet.

★ Think recycling. Every experience can be recycled if you keep your eyes, ears and your mind open. So what if it does all go pear-shaped? You can always write a bestselling book about your experiences!

★ Think other opportunities. Whatever you do, keep your eyes open. Good opportunities tend to come when you least expect them, but you do have to be open and receptive to them when they pop up. Save up every skill, experience and facts you learn en route: you never know when they'll come in handy.

★ Think networking. People in business have long memories when it comes to talent. Even if you weren't right today, make sure you create a good impression. You never know when the perfect opportunity might come along.

Phone a Friend

When you have an idea it's vital to get advice to develop it. Lots of the people interviewed in this book mention mentors – people who helped nurture an idea.

BANK ON THIS
Some Facts About Mentors

★ Mentors help you to achieve your goals. A mentor has three key qualities: time, knowledge and enthusiasm.

★ This doesn't mean you only approach people who aren't busy. Very busy people are often better time managers and better at finding the time to offer help.

★ Knowledge is important, though. It's no good asking someone for help just because they're older and quite keen. To get to the top you're going to need proper insights, expertise and guidance from someone who's been there and done it themselves.

★ Your mum, dad and teachers mentor you already, but before you ask them for more help, work out what type of advice you're looking for: write a shopping list. If it's financial or marketing you need to speak to someone with those backgrounds. Do your parents work in those areas? Has your teacher got contacts in business? If the answer is 'no', you'll need to look elsewhere.

★ You can write to top names to ask for tips or advice or you could approach local businesses (although make sure they don't pinch your ideas!).

★ A mentor can offer all sorts of help. You need to discuss how available they'll be and what they'll do before you start the mentoring. They could give you regular advice, be on tap when you have a problem or it could be a one-off conversation when you need answers. Always remember, time is expensive, so never take your mentor for granted. Turn up on time for meetings and try never to cancel unless absolutely necessary. Ring when you say you will and always acknowledge emails. And remember to thank your mentor.

There are plenty of organizations out there that can provide help to young guns. Think carefully about anyone who asks you to pay for advice. There is plenty of free back-up.

BANK ON THIS LOT
Sources of Good Advice:

Enterprise Insight

This is a government body that aims to encourage enterprise in young people. It runs a Make Your Mark Campaign with a great website, which includes practical tips as well as examples of inspiring success stories. There are links to loads of other organizations that can help with different aspects of the biz. See *www.starttalkingideas.org* It includes details of competitions and schemes you can get involved in and it also runs Enterprise Week. Visit the special website at *www.enterpriseweek.org*

Shell *Live*WIRE

A group that offers business advice for 16–30-year-olds and has helped 600,000 people thinking of starting their own business. There's a mentoring service for putting your questions to people who have already achieved big things in business, as well as online business kits for setting up your own outfit. They also run the Young Entrepreneur Awards and a competition for a grant. Visit their website at *www.shell-livewire.org*

Business Dynamics

They run courses for teenagers on getting businesses started. See *www.businessdynamics.org.uk*

Young Enterprise

They are the largest of the UK's business and education charities and have run new enterprise summer schools for 14–16-year-olds. They can link up with your school too. Find out more at *www.young-enterprise.org.uk*

Prince's Trust

Once you are over 18 the Prince's Trust could help you get a business up and running with grants and loans. They also provide grants for community projects to under-18s. See *www.princes-trust.org.uk*

Small Business Advice Centre

Its online advice service does what it says on the tin. Visit *www.smallbusinessadvice.org.uk*

Connexions Direct

Offer advice to young disabled people thinking of starting a business. See *www.connexions-direct.com*

Business Link

This is a bit adult-orientated, but it does have a directory of organizations in your area. See *www.businesslink.gov.uk*

Fashion Academy

Budding clothes designers might want to check out *www.fashionretailacademy.ac.uk*

BANK ON THIS

Tips on the Importance of Getting Support

'At primary level activities such as running a shop, making and selling biscuits, making presentations on project work in any subject, and team-based activities in whatever field are simple examples of enterprise and are also fun. If we can raise awareness and get involvement at this stage, enterprise becomes just as much as a learning continuum as maths or English.

'In my experience young people are prone to any number of mistakes when starting out. My advice to minimize them is simple. Do something that you are passionate about. Get started quickly before you talk yourself out of it. Take advice from others who have done it, but remember it is your business. Get back up when you get knocked down. Get the education you need first and never stop learning. If it stops being fun, sell it and do something else.

'Talk to people who can help and advise – friends, other young people with ideas, parents, teachers, youth group leaders, business people, bank managers, business-support agencies, particularly Business Link. Seek out useful websites. Don't be afraid to ask the 'idiot' questions. You can ask them far more easily as a teenager than later on.' – William Oxley, Young Person's Enterprise Forum

So, What's the Deal?

You've covered a lot of ground and there's no point trying to do everything at once. Don't let your motivation get zapped by the detail.

By now you should have a feel for whether you want to start a business, as well as an idea of what your project might be and how you might develop it.

Make sure you get your head round these key points:

★ Are you going to sell just a few homemade CDs or do you want to make the business a formal one?

★ What is going to go in your business plan?

★ Concentrate on taking small steps rather than trying to become a tycoon overnight.

★ Develop your basic business skills, like presenting and negotiating.

★ Can a mentor or business-support organization help?

★ How are you going to market, and ultimately sell, your product?

Maybe you think that you've got another skill or talent to make you a five-star-rated success. Learn to capitalize on it in our next chapter.

5.
HOW TO BE AN ENTERTAIN-AIRE

Can you sing, dance, act, write or make people laugh? Not everyone's got a head for business, maybe you've got a talent to perform instead. Maybe you just do it for fun now but your skills could be the source of a fabulous career too. By taking your raw talents and adding enthusiasm, energy, drive and a dollop of luck, you could make what is a hobby into a lifetime's work and passion. Who knows, you could even find fame.

To grab success in the world of entertainment you can expect a few knock-backs. But, if you have belief in yourself and have the ability plus the dedication, you'll learn to cope with all the hiccups and motivate yourself for success. When you see famous people gliding up the red carpet or strutting their stuff onstage, you're seeing the end result of loads of auditions, training, rehearsals and hard slog. They were so inspired by their goals and so revved up by their own talent that they saw that as part of the process.

This chapter will help you take your gifts and grow them, not by wildly chasing fame but by showing how to grab every opportunity and make the most of it. Find out too how some of the big stars got on the road to success, how they stayed true to their talents and continued to believe in themselves when the going got tough. You will also find out where to look for a helping hand with your talent.

The good news is that once you're on the way the sky is literally the limit. But, first, whatever you want to do, here are some things to start thinking about:

Think About Talent

OK, so all those reality TV stars got there with very little ability, but don't forget how quickly most of them slipped off the front pages once the programme was over. To have staying power you'll want to develop a real performing skill.

Think About Polishing Your Talent

It's best to aim high if you're going to market yourself. Being good is one thing, but being best is better. Write out a work plan. How good are you now and how good do you want to be? What will it take to make your skill or talent special? List your ideas for training, practising, watching other people or even rehearsing in a group or band.

Think Skill, Dedication and Passion

They are more important than the desire to simply be famous. It's vital to enjoy what you do. Most top performers found fame was just a by-product of doing what they loved best and it was that passion that kept them going when things were difficult.

Do Your Groundwork

Look for role models and performers who inspire you. Find out how they got there.

MILLI-MOUTH

'Talent is cheaper than table salt. What separates the talented individual from the successful one is a lot of hard work.' –
Stephen King, novelist

Chris Tarrant's face is known to millions of TV viewers and he knows a thing or two about making millionaires too. Here's how he made his name in the world of telly.

HOT SEAT:
CHRIS TARRANT

Fast facts

Who: *Presenter of TV's Who Wants To Be A Millionaire?*

Success factor: *Started out as a teacher but got his break on the box after sending letters to TV saying, 'This is your last chance to snap me up.' He later shot to fame on Saturday morning show Tiswas, became a radio DJ and has become a millionaire in his own right since landing his gig as a top game-show host.*

Trivia bite: *As a young man he once lived in a small van in the grounds of the school where he worked.*

Did you dream of being famous as a kid?

No, it never crossed my mind. I just wanted to play cricket for England!

Sometimes young people are told that making money is not what they should aim for. Is this true?

I think it's never a bad thing to have some money. It may not bring guaranteed happiness but it certainly helps and an awful lot of people's lives are very miserable because they just don't have enough money.

What's it like seeing people win a million?

There have been six million-pound winners now – well, five really, because one was a crook! Each time it has happened it is still hugely exciting. The atmosphere in the studio is fantastic and everybody – audience, crew, myself and obviously the contestants – are absolutely exhilarated. It happened about three months ago again and it was still as nerve tingling and exciting as ever. It still gives me a great buzz.

What was your biggest setback and how did you deal with it?

The break-up of my marriage. The pain for all concerned, particularly my kids, has been massively intensified by the relentless pressure from the gutter press. However, we have all come through the worst and are slowly getting things back together.

What pitfalls should young people watch out for on the road to stardom?

A lot of people promise a lot of things and don't mean them. The only real answer is to persevere but expect a lot of disappointment along the way. If you have genuine talent, are prepared to work hard and pester, pester, pester everybody you can, you will make it.

What would you do with a spare million pounds?

Probably share it among the various charities that I am patron of.

Any words of encouragement for readers looking to make it?

Good luck – look forward to seeing you on TV or stage!

MILLI-FACT

Many of the world's highest-earning entertainers are dead. In 2005–06 legendary singer Elvis's estate earned over £22 million. Yet he died in 1977!

Have I Really Got Talent?

A good starting point is to watch other performers in your field to check the competition. Then work out whether you've got what it takes. Be very analytical. Most top celebs are good at several things. Kylie, Madonna and Christina Aguilera can all dance as well as sing. They look good too. Kate Moss and Naomi don't just have beautiful faces, they have perfect figures and they can sashay down a catwalk and sell clothes because they move well. Most bands write their own songs.

Ask yourself these questions, and be honest with the answer:

★ Would I pay to see myself perform?

★ Why? What makes me special?

MILLI-MOUTH

Working out whether you have got talent can be hard because it's difficult to be objective. But take heart from two of the world's top entertainers who once didn't rate themselves at all.

❝As a teenager I was so insecure. I was the type of guy that never fitted in because he never dared to choose. I was convinced I had absolutely no talent at all. For nothing. And that thought took away all my ambition too.❞ – *Johnny Depp*, Pirates of the Caribbean *star*

❝It was such a turning point to find that I had a talent and I had something to contribute, somewhere.❞– *Pop star Gwen Stefani*

BRAIN BOX
Defining Your Talent

★ **Play to your strengths:** Work on what you're best at. Being different or unique is better than copying somebody else.

★ **Pick something you have the basic ingredients for:** Modelling agencies usually want very tall girls. Rock stars tend to be young. Actors don't usually have lisps or squeaky voices . . .

★ **Forget the BF (bathroom factor):** Everyone has 'bathroom talent'. Get in front of that mirror, suck in your tum and you could be the next Lily Cole. Grab the shower head and you can sing like George Michael. Reality check: none of the above needs to invite camera crews into their bathrooms to see them perform at their best. You have to be able to do it in front of an audience.

★ **Know all about your talent:** What is your pitch or range? What are your physical measurements? How well can you play musical instruments? What type of dance have you been trained for?

One thing is for sure: people are making it and becoming famous at a younger age than ever before, so you *do* have a chance.

MILLI-MOUTH
❛I'm beginning to think 12 is the new 20❜ –
X Factor *judge Simon Cowell*

Get Confident

Two of the biggest talent-nobblers around are shyness and lack of confidence. What if you are the next Robbie Williams but you're so wary of meeting people that your great talent is a secret between you and the bathroom mirror? Well, we're looking at two key options here, either you:

(a) Give up, and let the more confident types get all the glory.

(b) Work hard to overcome the problem and let your talent shine through. Why should it only be the confident kids out there onstage? After all, it's easier to have talent and overcome shyness than have the singing voice of a strangulated hamster but lots of confidence.

Keeping a Balance

Draw a straight line. Write 'confident' in the middle and 'shy' at the left end. Take a look at the empty right end for a moment. This is where you'd write the words 'over-confident'. Can you have too much confidence? Of course, and it can be just as much of a problem as shyness. The performing world is full of people whose confidence outstrips their talent. It's great to think you're good but it's not always good to think you're great. Over-confidence can create arrogance, which means you can't evaluate your own worth. It can mean you stop improving, training and working on your skills. Don't go there! Talking yourself up is fine but being a big head is never a winner.

Listen carefully to what people say about your level of talent and then make your own judgement. Work out if they're being polite, letting you down gently or, just possibly, don't really know what they're talking about.

BANK ON THIS

Three Stars Who Were Told They'd Never Make It

Liam Gallagher, the Oasis front man, was warned off music. He once recalled: 'Schooldays were the worst days of my life. My music teacher once said to me: "You don't have a clue about music. You don't even know about scales."'

Colin Farrell, now a Hollywood star, was once told by *X Factor* judge Louis Walsh that he'd never make it in showbiz when he auditioned for Boyzone. Louis says, 'I told him he was wasting his time.'

Victoria Beckham also struggled to get picked for auditions as a teenager before landing her place in the Spice Girls.

Shying away from shyness

Want to hoover that shy gene out of your life for good? First you need to understand why you're too afraid to look anyone – even the family pet – in the eye.

Shyness is a rush of fear we all feel when we're with people we don't know very well. Guess what? It's natural. Very few animals would survive if they went around hugging other animals and greeting them like they were old friends all the time, even though they hadn't been introduced. Nature makes us wary. It's just that some of us stay too wary for too long and it becomes a hurdle. Symptoms of shyness vary, but include little eye contact, head held down, hiding behind hair, giggling, blushing, getting sweaty, stammering and avoiding situations you find daunting.

'Oh my God! I've got all of those,' you may be saying. But hang on! Some good news: many people you see on TV or cinema screens are shy. Leona Lewis won *X Factor*, yet she was shy. Shy people *can* get on. They just find ways to hide their shyness. It's a very common trait among successful performers and business people. They found ways of working with it – and so can you.

Even better than good news: it's self-inflicted! So unlike the flu or acne or hairy feet, you do have a choice. Shyness is a bit like a mangy, snagged and stained old cardigan that's lying at the end of your bed every morning when you wake up. It's you who decides to wear it all day. Nobody makes you; it was your option.

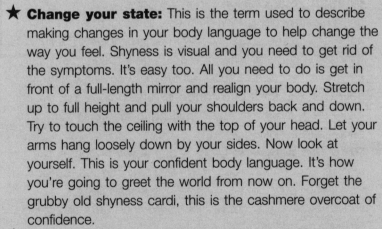

BRAIN BOX
Lose Your Shyness

★ **Change your state:** This is the term used to describe making changes in your body language to help change the way you feel. Shyness is visual and you need to get rid of the symptoms. It's easy too. All you need to do is get in front of a full-length mirror and realign your body. Stretch up to full height and pull your shoulders back and down. Try to touch the ceiling with the top of your head. Let your arms hang loosely down by your sides. Now look at yourself. This is your confident body language. It's how you're going to greet the world from now on. Forget the grubby old shyness cardi, this is the cashmere overcoat of confidence.

★ **Stop fiddling and twiddling:** These are self-comfort gestures, but they make you look nervy. If you fiddle with jewellery or hair, tie the hair back and leave the jewellery at home.

★ **Avoid body barriers:** When you fold your arms it's like creating a wall between you and the rest of the world. This is fine if you want to feed your shyness but not if you want to overcome it. Avoid body barriers, especially if they involve bags or papers, and keep your hands away from your face too.

★ **Give them the eye:** Shy eyes look shifty, but don't overdo the staring either, or you could just look mad. Start counting how long you can hold a person's gaze for. Instead of glancing up and looking away quickly, try doubling or tripling the time. Three seconds won't kill you but it will make you look more in control.

★ **Keep your hair off your face:** It's the handiest of cover-ups.

★ **Change your words:** When we get shy our conversations get gunky, then dry up altogether. So why not create some script for use in emergencies? Think of things you can say when the going gets tough. Can you ask the other person about an interest you know they've got? Can you think of a couple of funny things that might make them laugh? Is there anything in the news that people are speaking about?

★ **Drop the baggage:** Drop all that heavy baggage, like worries about your looks. You have two choices: either you sit on your bum all day wishing you looked like a supermodel or you get off your bum and start capitalizing on your own strengths.

★ **Tell yourself you're good:** Talk yourself up (but only in the mirror).

★ **Push yourself day by day:** To learn any skill you have to *do it*! If you want to be a better runner, you run. If you want to learn how to drive, you drive. So if you want to be more confident you do confidence exercises. It's best to set your own mini-tests because only you know what will stretch you. Here are some examples, though:

1. Speaking up in class. Being the first to ask a question or make a point.
2. Sitting in the front row instead of hiding at the back.
3. Making your own point instead of agreeing with everyone.
4. Speaking to a shop assistant. When you're at the till try a bit of small talk.
5. Phoning a company and asking for advice or information.
6. Saying 'thank you' to a compliment instead of rubbishing it.
7. Introducing yourself to strangers (in a safe environment!).
8. Phoning friends and relatives rather than texting.

OK, you've got talent. You're feeling pretty good about it. It's time to tell the world.

But how do you go about getting your talent out there? The ways of getting on often overlap. After all, you might have more than one talent and some of the same tips that apply to singing also apply to acting.

But let's try and break things down a bit. First, telly – everyone's watched it. But how do you get into TV and film industries so that you end up on the screen?

Acting Up: Getting on the Stage and Screen

Yep, you've heard it before (this super-success lark is no cakewalk): there's no application form to be the next Fearne Cotton, Ant and Dec or Orlando Bloom. What you need to do is get your face in front of people – the right people. Then you need some luck.

BANK ON THIS
Ways In

★ **Back to school:** There are special showbiz schools where you learn to perform as well as do all the normal schoolwork. Examples include BRIT school and the Sylvia Young Theatre School.
See *www.drama.ac.uk* for more.

★ **Get a job:** as a runner for a TV show and hope someone spots your talent. Pick something appropriate. A stint on *Antiques Roadshow* may pay fewer dividends than something starring Ant and Dec. Consider volunteering to work for a venue in your spare time and be prepared to do anything from serving drinks and selling tickets to booking talent. It pays to be around the scene and to make contacts.

★ **Be on the lookout:** Scan trade publications like *The Stage* and *The Spotlight* website *www.spotlight.com* Also check out websites looking for people to be on shows, like *www.beonscreen.com* The big TV channels all have sections about which shows you can apply to be on and which are always looking for new talent. The website *www.bbc.co.uk/newtalent* is a useful place to start.

★ **Auditions:** There are lots of different types of audition. Try school or local drama groups. You could even join the queues for programmes like *X Factor*. But, remember that even if you're the right age, your chances of getting in are slim and you could be letting yourself in for more than you bargained for. The reality TV spotlight can be unforgiving. They aren't the only shows out there looking for young stars – *Junior Mastermind* for example.

★ **Train to be a presenter:** There are courses out there but they cost and don't guarantee jobs. You're probably better off doing work experience at your local TV station, then getting a job as a runner or researcher. Good presenters are as rare as hens' teeth. The best ones, like Dermot O'Leary, might make it look easy, but never be fooled, that's part of his genius! Bear in mind too that these days a lot of people on TV trained to be experts in something else first, like antiques or property.

★ **Think outside the box:** There are more ways than ever to get your stuff out there. Do a video for YouTube and don't dismiss holiday camps, educational theatre, pantomimes, revue shows, local drama clubs and karaoke competitions. You could even become an extra.

★ **Get a showreel together:** Get a friend to film a stage performance and get it in front of an agent.

What's it like, taking your first steps to get on screen? Here's one teen star who knows . . .

HOT SEAT:
RUPERT GRINT

Fast facts

Who: *Plays ginger-haired hero Ron Weasley in the* Harry Potter *movies.*

Success factor: *Went from school plays to Potter fame after sending a home video to the film's casting department. He was still only 13 when* Harry Potter and the Philosopher's Stone *hit cinemas and, as well as starring in all the Potter films, has also acted in* Driving Lessons *and* Thunderpants.

Trivia bite: *Has a real-life fear of spiders, just like his HP character.*

Can you remember when you wanted to become an actor?

I did a primary-school talent show as Mystic Meg. I was only about 7 at the time but I think this is when I really first realized I enjoyed acting.

How did you get the part in *Harry Potter*?

I saw a request put out on the afternoon show *Newsround* inviting people to audition for Ron, Harry and Hermione. I sent off a letter, had no reply, so my mum and I made a video, where I dressed up as my ex-drama teacher and sang a made-up rap about how much I wanted the part of Ron. Although it seems quite embarrassing now, at the time it was good fun and I desperately wanted a chance to audition, and it seemed to work.

How would you advise aspiring young actors?

To really have faith in yourself, to lose yourself in the character so you lose your inhibitions and totally become the person you're portraying, which will give you the confidence to succeed and give it your very best shot.

How important is it to have supportive parents and friends?

Extremely important. I wouldn't have been able to do the video without my mum's support and help. Also, having the back-up allowed me to concentrate on what I really wanted to do, knowing I had my family and friends to back me up and help at all times – no matter what!

Has it been scary becoming famous at such a young age? What do you think are the biggest pitfalls to watch out for?

Not scary but quite daunting sometimes with the press, etc. Also, not being able to go anywhere anonymously sometimes can be hard – especially with my hair! But I wouldn't say it was scary, for the most part it's really exciting and fun. As far as pitfalls, well, really just to not forget who you are, and who is important and genuine in your life.

Do you have to be a bit of a businessman too?

In some ways yes, or at least you need to look forward and plan for the future, as who knows what life has in store! I've also been helped by having good support and advice from not only friends and family but professionals as well.

What luxuries have you bought?

I have a great set of golf clubs. I have recently passed my driving test so I have a new Mini One and an old American 1950 Chevy pick-up which I am doing up at the moment.

Which actor who you have met have you been most in awe of?

I met Robin Williams at the first US premiere of *Harry Potter and the Philosopher's Stone*. He was really nice and very funny. Unfortunately my granddad was sitting next to me at the time and kept doing Mrs

Doubtfire impressions! Embarrassing, but nevertheless at age 12 it was quite a moment.

How do you relax off-set?
I love playing golf. I like playing Need for Speed on Xbox, and I also like to draw cartoons.

What's your ultimate ambition as an actor?
I would like to play a very nasty villain at some stage, but my ambition is to keep working – doing as many different and varied things as possible!

RUPERT'S TOP TIPS
★ Be determined about what you want to achieve.
★ Have a good sense of humour and have fun.
★ Respect everyone you work with.

Will I Need an Agent?
You don't need one, but if you have a showreel an agent will help you find work – that's their job. For the better acting and TV jobs, your best chance is to have an agent pitching for you. They work on commission and shouldn't charge you to register with them. Contact the Agents' Association (*www.agents-uk.com*).

Once you have done some work you might want to become a member of the actors' union, Equity (*www.equity.org.uk*), that runs a job-information service.

Strike a Note: Getting Musical

There are loads of ways of getting a musical career started, depending on what part of the business suits you.

BANK ON THIS

Form a band: It takes the pressure off trying to make it on your own, though you'd better make sure they are good mates. We've all seen too many messy splits when bandmates fall out. Get gigs anywhere you can – even the school disco if necessary.

Make a demo: Choose your best three tracks and send them to record companies. Make sure the quality's good or they will go straight in the bin.

Go direct to your audience: The Arctic Monkeys got their start by making their songs free online. Download sales mean it's now possible (like the band Koopa proved) to get a top-40 hit without being signed to a record label.

TV shows and competitions: Yes, you can audition for the *X Factor* and become the next Will Young. But there are other competitions out there too, such as the BBC's *Young Musician of the Year*.

Here's a singing star who built herself a smash-hit career slowly and sensibly . . .

HOT SEAT:
KATIE MELUA

Fast facts
Who: *Great singer who released her first album,* Call Off the Search, *at 19.*

Success factor: *Her second album went platinum four times and she has become the highest-selling female artist in the UK, worth around £5 million according to* The Sunday Times Rich List *in 2006.*

Trivia bite: *Went to the BRIT School for the Performing Arts, where she was spotted by songwriter Mike Batt. She also appeared on a spoof ITV show called* Stars Up Their Nose, *aged 15.*

Were you determined to be a famous singer?

Not really; I loved music as a hobby and rather than wanting to be famous and successful I just truly loved the music. When I was 15 I decided to take it more seriously, even if I never made it professionally. I saved up and bought myself a home recording system and spent all my spare time experimenting with music

How did you get in front of the right people?

I went to the BRIT School, where I was taught about the music industry as a business, from production to writing to singing and recording . . . basically a broad base. It gave me the opportunity to get better at what I what I was already doing. Then Mike Batt, who is now my producer and manager, came to one of the school's open days and things went from there.

When did you feel you had really made it?

I suppose the defining moment was definitely playing with Queen in front of Nelson Mandela. I don't think of having 'made it' . . . it's more a case of 'making it'.

What attitude did you have? And was that important?

I love what I do because I do it for the music and the creative side of things. The fame side of what I do is all fake. If you're not into what you do for the right reasons you'll never have enough passion to really be all you want to be, to be fulfilled.

Did you have to choose between study and music?

I was fortunate that I didn't have to choose between study and college, both were able to be combined. Education is so important if you make sure that you get a lot out of it. I wouldn't be where I am if I hadn't had the education; bettering yourself is something I love doing. And once you've learnt the rules you can learn how to break them.

What did your friends think when you were trying to make it?

Most of my friends are musicians. I never tried to 'make it' so they never thought of me like that. I don't really talk about it that much; even now we talk about normal things, not what I've done that day and where I've been. At the end of the day it is my job and I want to hear about their day as much as they want to hear about mine – that's how it should be!

Have you ever found your age meant you weren't taken seriously?

Occasionally, people think they can patronize you. At the beginning there are a lot of things to learn so you accept what you're taught and learn from it, making sure the more you know the more you make sure your point is heard; knowledge is power.

What was your biggest setback and how did you deal with it?

I'm signed to a small indie company. We have to 'compete' with mainstream record companies and mainstream music that is heard on radio, seen on TV all the time and seen in the press a lot. It can still be hard for an independent company to get media exposure or even to have a CD stocked in the stores. Just as it was hard for me to get a deal with a mainstream company at the beginning, it was hard for them to take a chance on me – there are so many positives to being signed to an indie that for me they definitely outweigh the negatives.

What luxuries do you spoil yourself with?
I like guitars and CDs. I'm not a big shopper, really. I spend money on music but I hate wasting money. Due to my Eastern European roots I know the value of money and I'd hate to spend hundreds on a pair of shoes when I know it could feed a whole family for months.

What is the biggest risk for young people starting out?
Caring about what you do and working hard is so important. If you want something it's not going to land in your lap. The risk is that it's easy to be naive and have misguided preconceptions about how it's going to be. You need to have a realistic view about what the job/career will entail. If you aren't going to be able to be away from your loved ones for long periods of time, it will be hard to be in a band and tour. You can also get taken advantage of; you have to know what you want from it all and stick to it.

What do you love about what you do?
I love knowing your hard work is productive. You can see results and you get feedback through sales and fans. It's so rewarding.

What should teenagers do if they start making a lot of money? Can you have too much too soon?
Yes, you can have too much too soon. It can cause more problems than it fixes. You have to be sensible. Reward yourself when you've worked hard, but it's good to be aware it could be gone any minute.

Knowing things can't last forever is a real incentive to be that little bit more sensible. I'm not that much of a big spender anyway.

What's the funniest thing that's happened to you onstage?
I was doing a concert in Germany when I saw a guy collapse in the audience. I had to continue with the song, but at the end, once he'd been taken off in a stretcher by an ambulance, I – without thinking what the next song was – told the entire audience I wanted to dedicate the next song to him. I looked down at the set list which I keep by my feet and, to my horror, I saw the song was 'Just Like Heaven'! I didn't introduce the song with its name, I just started playing, hoping the song I was dedicating to him wasn't true! I've heard since he's fine.

KATIE'S TOP TIPS
★ Go with your gut instinct.
★ Be honest and stay true to yourself.
★ Work hard. It sounds obvious, but no one got successful by not trying hard and having motivation and passion.

Do You Need Formal Training or Even Be Able to Read Music?
No, not necessarily. Obviously it's going to help. But Beatles singer Paul McCartney couldn't read sheet music when he came up with some of the biggest hits ever.

There are many ways to make music. The original *Doctor Who* theme tune was recorded by sampling electronic equipment. Murray Gold, who adapted it for the new series, reckons you don't need any formal training, citing composers like Lionel Bart, who didn't write his songs down. He says: 'Anyone can contribute to music.'

BRAIN BOX

How to Get Through an Audition

★ Turn up on time or early, especially if you know you'll have to queue.

★ Don't waste energy mucking about beforehand.

★ Look good while you wait. Sometimes talent-spotters are sent to check out the queuers.

★ Walk in well. You're being auditioned from the moment you step into the room.

★ Don't tell them you're nervous or point out any negatives.

★ Warm up before you go in, especially if you're singing.

★ Sip lukewarm water, not hot or iced, to lubricate your throat.

★ Avoid dairy products, like milky drinks, before your audition.

★ Always read the brief carefully. Don't turn up to an audition for *Evita* prepared for *The Sound of Music*.

★ Take a 'moment' before you start.

★ Impress with your personality as well as your talent.

★ Keep your outfit simple and let them see the real you.

★ One chaperone is OK but don't make it a day out for your entire family.

★ Listen to feedback. Don't interrupt or argue.

★ Keep your dignity: blubbing is for lightweights.

★ Be original – judges get fed up hearing songs from *Annie*.

★ Act your age. If you're young, don't sing a piece from *Cabaret* or *Chicago*.

★ Be resilient. You might go to ten auditions a day and get turned down for all of them. But the more you go to the more experience you get and the greater your chances of getting a thumbs-up next time.

MILLI-FACT

To get a number-one record, experts reckon you have got to sell around 133,000 copies a week. A platinum single is when you sell 300,000 in total, and for a platinum album you have to flog 600,000.

Remember: you don't have to be a pop star or in a band to be a famous musician. There are many areas in the music business. Find the one that best suits you and your talents. Classical music (singing or playing an instrument)? World music? Writing lyrics? Composing? Perhaps being a DJ and mixing other people's music?

Singer Katherine Jenkins says chasing fame isn't the answer. It's about finding the musical clothes that fit. Success is about hitting the right notes, not just counting them in your wallet.

HOT SEAT:
KATHERINE JENKINS

Fast facts

Who: *Britain's bestselling classical singer of all time.*

Success factor: *At 13 she became BBC Welsh Choirgirl of the Year and went on to study at the Royal Academy of Music. By 23, she had signed a seven-figure deal – the largest in UK classical recording history.*

Trivia bite: *Katherine has been to Iraq to sing to the British army.*

As a child, did you want to be famous or did it just happen?

I always wanted to be a singer but not necessarily famous. Of course, now I realize that the two things come hand in hand. However, it scares me now that young people want to be famous without actually achieving anything first. We should be telling them that it's all about hard work and determination.

Where did you get your inspiration? What made you decide that singing was for you?

It was just something inside me. Singing is all I've wanted to do since I was four years old and took part in my first talent show. Of course, there have been people who have inspired me, like Madonna, Maria Callas, Judy Garland, Placido Domingo and many, many more.

How did you get your big break?

I made a demo with a friend of mine (Steve DuBerry) when I was 22 which got passed through a friend of a friend to Universal Music. I got a call out of the blue inviting me to their office for a meeting. During the meeting they said they would like to hear me sing live and so they arranged a showcase for me where I performed to four bosses of the record company, who looked completely uninterested. When I finished they said, 'Thanks, we'll let you know.' I went home feeling like I'd blown it but in less than an hour I had a call saying they were offering me a six-album deal! I cried all day!

You have come a long way at a young age. Have you ever found your age problematic in terms of being taken seriously?

No, I haven't. I've always been very involved in all the decision-making and I've always wanted to learn about the business side of things. Also, I realize that my voice will not be completely developed for a few years so I think I've only attempted to do things that I'm ready for. Opera is something I'd love to do when I'm around 30.

Was there any benefit to starting young?

I'm really pleased that all this happened to me at the age it did. I had just graduated from the Royal Academy of Music and I'd had time to do the 'student thing'. I learnt a lot of invaluable lessons there about how to look after my voice, etc. and the friends that I made there are now trying to get their break, which only highlights to me again just how lucky I have been. All this has taught me to enjoy it all and not take it for granted.

What do you love about what you do?

The singing, the connection with the audience, meeting amazing people, going to places I've always wanted to visit, singing with people I've admired all my life and sharing it all with my family.

What luxuries do you spoil yourself with?

I'm a shoe-aholic and I love handbags! I've just become the International Ambassador for Mont Blanc, which really helps my bag addiction as they have really gorgeous bags and I always get the new ones before they've even come out.

What ambitions do you have left?

I'd love to play the role of Carmen one day, sing with Placido Domingo and Andrea Bocelli and win a Grammy. I think it's always really important to have something to aim for.

What would you say is the secret of your success and what is the biggest risk?

I had really good advice at the start, which was to always be yourself. It's going to be a very hard act to keep up if you don't! I'm genuinely a girly girl. I love hair, make-up, etc. and so my record company have not had to make up an image for me that doesn't reflect the real me. My career means so much to me and I'm not really a risk taker, so I can't really think of any big risks.

What is the best thing about being famous and can you have too much too soon?

The best thing for me is being able to share all this with my family. I love taking them away with me, inviting them to the Classical Brits and introducing them to people they love. I once introduced my mum to Sir Tom Jones and I thought she was going to faint! Having too much too soon? I think it all depends on your attitude. I don't see why any of this needs to change a person. Of course, people want to treat you differently, but I want to be able to go home to Wales and be the same person I was at the start of all this.

KATHERINE'S TOP TIPS

★ Try to involve yourself in as much local music as you can. Join any choir, enter competitions and try to get involved with theatre groups, like amateur operatic societies. It's all great experience that will help you later on.

★ Get a good singing teacher. Always ask around for a good recommendation or call the Associated Board of Music to see if they have any recommendations in your area.

★ Try to get into a music college and make a demo to send in to the record labels. Also, believe in yourself. My dad always told me that if I worked hard enough and believed in myself I would make it. Thanks, Dad!

Write On: Making Words Your Future

You've probably heard of *Harry Potter* author, J. K. Rowling. She wrote most of the first HP book in a cafe. It might seem like a pretty humble place to start, but within a few years her super scribblings had sent shock waves round the world. It's amazing what you can achieve armed with a cup of tea and a pen.

While TV and music get the most publicity, writing is another brilliant way to start pouring out all your creative juices. All the tools for writing your own book, short stories, poetry or plays are probably within a few feet of where you're sitting now.

After all, you're reading a book. Why not write one?

BANK ON THIS

Writing Tips

★ Get something down on your computer. Sitting gazing at a blank screen, waiting for inspiration to happen, is a waste of time and sure to cause writer's block. Write any thoughts or ideas – you can always edit them later.

★ Carry a notebook. Writers pick up plot and character ideas, and even words they like, in the way most of us pick up bargains in a sale. They write down anything and everything in a notebook, then recycle later.

★ Don't worry about coming up with the most original idea in the world ever. You'd never start. Of course, you can't go around copying other people's work, but it's fine to use stuff you read and see as inspiration. You can get snatches of plots from soaps on TV, problem pages in your magazine, friends' gossip – the world's full of real-life storylines!

★ Keep to what you know. You might not think your life's full of drama, but if you write well about things you've experienced or know about, you'll entertain better than tripping down fantasy alley.

★ 'Read' the world around you. Start to see everything in literary terms. If your friend has a problem, imagine what he/she's thinking or feeling about it. What could the outcome be? What if it all went wrong? What other characters of stories might get involved as a result?

★ Start to put a plot together. But first pick up some books that you think might have been written in the same way as the one in your head. Get an idea of size, chapter length and layout.

★ A plot isn't just one idea. All good novels have different themes running around and through the main plot. Ditto with characters. Take a book you like and count how many characters it has – you might be surprised!

★ It's not always vital to write the whole book before you sell it. Often a book is sold on an outline – character details and descriptions, chapter headings – and two complete chapters to show writing style.

★ It's good to approach an agent first. A good agent will send your outline to the right type of publishers and negotiate a much better deal if it gets accepted.

★ Listen to your agent. They know what they're doing and they know what sells.

★ Be patient. Most top books were turned down loads before they got published.

★ If a novel seems daunting, why not try short stories for local magazines and newspapers? You have to start somewhere and seeing your name in print is a buzz.

★ Publish yourself: start a blog or set up a MySpace page.

This is how one brilliant young author got her inspiration.

HOT SEAT:
CECELIA AHERN

Fast facts

Who: *Bestselling author who had her first smash hit when she was 21.*

Success factor: *Her first novel, PS, I love You, was printed in 50 countries and she sold the movie rights too. She has now written three more books and is still in her early twenties.*

Trivia bite: *Her dad happens to be prime minister of Ireland. Find out more about Cecelia at* www.cecelia-ahern.com

How young were you when you knew you wanted to write books? Did you have any other career in mind?

I always knew from a very young age that I wanted to do a communications course. I read about it one day and it struck me straight away as an ideal course for me. It involved a more creative side, which was always my stronger side. It included film and television studies, creative writing and radio broadcasting among many other things. Not being a huge fan of school, it was the first time that I realized that studying could actually be something that I enjoyed doing rather than just having to try to get through. I had always been fascinated by and was a huge fan of television and I'd had the opportunity to watch behind-the-scenes action when I'd accompany my dad to television studios for his Sunday interviews. That spurred on my desire to work in that field.

Funnily enough I never knew that I wanted to write as a career. It was always something that I loved doing by myself, for myself; I was never interested in showing my work to anybody else and found writing to be a personal and very private experience. Most of what I was writing was very personal anyway – diaries, poetry – but it was all about my life and so I wasn't very keen on letting anybody else read my most innermost thoughts. When I was 14 I wrote my first book, *Beans on Toast and a Bottle of Beer*, which I never finished, but it was about a 16-year-old just growing up. They say your first novel is autobiographical so I'm assuming that one was! I showed that work to my mom, who was so encouraging. She told a teacher of mine at that year's parent-teacher meeting, which absolutely mortified me and I refused to show him my work, though he was hugely encouraging and kept asking. After school I received a degree in journalism and media communications and I was planning to do a masters in film production, but after two days I got the idea for my first book, *PS, I Love You*, and decided to leave to write it full time. It was *PS, I Love You* that turned everything around for me, that turned what was a hobby I was incredibly passionate about into a career.

Did you choose to be a writer or did it choose you?

I always say that writing chooses you. When I get an idea it's when I'm not searching for one. When I write, I don't know where the sentences, the characters, the stories all come from. I feel like they just arrive one day and announce themselves to me and I have no choice but to put pen to paper. I think that's what makes a writer a writer, when they feel compelled to put pen to paper. They don't just want to write a story, they feel a story too and become so surrounded by the thoughts in their head they have to release it to the world on paper! Lots of people want to write books but I think it's the books that want to be written that are most successful.

Do you ever get lonely as a writer or are you happy working by yourself?

I am very happy working alone and I think that if you want to be a writer it's vital that you're comfortable with that. I think what makes me so comfortable with it is that I'm never really alone. I spend hours on end running conversations through my head, creating atmospheres, tasting, smelling and seeing far more than is in the room I'm working in. I find that when I'm finished writing, the last thing I want to do is to jump into another conversation with someone, as my mind has been so active. I'm lucky enough to have the best of both worlds because when I'm writing, I'm totally alone and then when I'm promoting, I'm travelling all over the world meeting so many lovely people that I never get a moment alone!

Do you have any special qualities?

I think with regards to personal qualities it's important to be passionate about what you do. It doesn't matter what you do, as long as you have a love for it you will give it all the time and hard work it needs. Dedication and hard work are very, very important!

Does being young help or is it ever a problem?

When I got my first publishing deal I was so surprised by the reaction to my age. Some people couldn't believe how someone so young could have written a story about love and loss. I've never ever felt in my entire life that somebody younger than me could have less knowledge about any kind of emotion. If you're human, you feel. If you can write, you can put those feelings into words and so I say, never ever let age be an issue with writing.

If a book had been turned down, would you have quit?

No, I wouldn't have. For me, writing is pure enjoyment. It's not about having books on a shelf or in charts (though they are wonderful bonuses!), writing is something that I would do regardless of book deals, but I am so thankful I have the opportunity to do it full time; it really is a dream job. That is so important for people who want to become writers: there may be rejections, but remember that for every person who dislikes your work there are so many more who may love it, so keep going!

CECELIA'S TOP TIPS

★ Find your own voice. Don't repeat what is already on the shelves, because when I'm reading it's not just the writing that appeals to me but the voice too. I'm never afraid to be different because playing it safe means that you sometimes lose out in exploring something that could be so wonderful and something no one else has covered before.

★ It's also important to have readers to give you that advice and encouragement that you need. My mom was a huge encouragement to me as she was the first person to read *PS, I Love You*. She also was the person who first suggested I try to get it published and even went looking for an agent for me to send it to. Getting the feedback from readers is so exciting and encouraging; it spurs me on to the finish line!

MILLI-FACT

A poll of teenagers in 2005 showed that a third of them had written their own online content.

What if I Can't Think of a Story?

You can write about anything. Here's someone who made it as a cookery writer – and is well on the way to being one of the top celebrity chefs of the future too.

HOT SEAT:
SAM STERN

Fast facts

Who: *Teenage chef who has stormed the book charts with his unique brand of cool cooking tips.*

Success factor: *Brought out his first book, Cooking Up a Storm, at 15 and has since starred on TV shows like Blue Peter. He's got his own show in the pipeline too.*

Trivia bite: *Check out Sam's website for more stuff about him and his recipes:* www.samstern.co.uk

When did you first get interested in cooking?

I've always been into it. My mum just sorta got me helping out when I was little. And I loved it. I remember the smell of her famous treacle bread when she opened the oven. I started out kneading dough. Making biscuits with her. The usual stuff, but just kept on doing it. My brother and sisters are all older than me so they'd be in the kitchen too. By the time I was about 9 I was doing roast chicken and other big meals. Now I love experimenting with food and coming up with my own stuff, like seeing what's in the fridge and seeing what I can do with it or taking a recipe and changing it a bit to try to improve it. Or, with a classic recipe, just getting it right. I love cooking for my mates and with my older brother.

What made you realize that it could be a career not a hobby and did you have a clear plan in your head?

I just love it, plus I wanted to inspire other kids to cook. It wasn't really a career move. By the time I was, like, 12 my brother was texting home from uni asking for our family recipes. He cooks too. Plus my mates were coming round, staying to eat and liking it. A lot of them don't eat well at home or there isn't the food in and they can't cook for themselves, plus their parents work late so there's nobody in to cook for them or maybe their parents can't cook anyway. So it just all sort of came together and it made sense to make a cookbook. There wasn't anything out there like that. It was a huge gap in the market and I thought, why not! I had to go to a meeting with Walker Books before they bought the idea – they wanted to see what I was like. I was shaking all through it but it worked out. We got a contract but didn't think much would happen. It didn't sell very fast at first because nobody knew who I was and nobody knew where to look for the books. In the kids' section? Teens? Or cookery? But then we got some good publicity and the press got interested because I am a teen voice talking to teens. It all just happened, but I guess it's because the message is important. And I thought: 'Well, if it makes a difference then I'd better do all the scary stuff like TV because it could definitely help kids.' And now it's become a mission. I've learnt so much more about food since I started doing it and realize how it's key to so much. I don't know if it's a career yet, but it's a big part of my life alongside education. It's important to keep studying because you never know what will happen – plus it helps. I study politics at A level and that ties up. Now the first book has been translated into 12 different languages and we've got the website, which gets loads of hits from teens so it's all working out.

Which TV chefs do you look up to and why?
Rick Stein. He goes to find local fresh organic produce and he's really passionate in a sincere way. I like the fact that he goes out to find his food heroes – people who grow or make great stuff. Hugh Fearnley-Whittingstall too. I love the way he uses every bit of the animal and grows his own stuff. Jamie Oliver, for all he has done to make cooking cool and the school-food campaign. Also Antony Worrall Thompson is a hero. I cooked with him on the BBC *Good Food Show* last year and he was awesome – really supportive and

funny. It was nerve wracking being in front of a huge live audience but he made it all right, and he didn't have to do that.

You have said you don't want to do it just for the fame and money. What are your ambitions?

I'm not too sure at the moment. I think there will be a TV show at some point but there are definitely another two books in the pipeline. The TV will happen – it's just a matter of finding what I want to do with a programme and what would be good. It's really important to only do the right things, where you can have as much control as possible. I've been offered TV shows by about 30 different production companies and when you are young you can get exploited. The media can use you, then dump you. So you have to be a bit sceptical. Don't just do something for the money or some fake celebrity. It's got to be real. I definitely want to do something with food in the future, though.

What's your ultimate luxury item?

The thing that I'm working towards is a Mercedes McLaren SLR – it's my dream car! It's a bit on the expensive side, but I'll have it one day. It's my screensaver.

What's your funniest cooking disaster?

I was making pasta for the first time on my own. You have to dig a well in the flour before you put the eggs in. I didn't dig the well deep enough though and the eggs went all over the floor, it was a very sticky situation.

SAM'S TOP TIPS

★ Be open-minded: give everything a go.
★ Be patient: it might not work out first time.
★ Whatever you do, use your own voice and make sure you love it.

What About All the Other Stuff?

There are loads of other ways to be a star. While it'd be difficult to explain how to turn your talent for playing the kazoo while pedalling backwards into a money-making wheeze, here are a few tips you may be interested in.

Modelling

BANK ON HER

Lily Cole: The red-haired beauty began her modelling career at 14, when she was spotted by a talent scout while walking through Covent Garden, London. Lily has managed to combine a career on the catwalk and fronting campaigns for Chanel and Prada with doing a degree at Cambridge University.

If you have got 'the look' then you may be spotted by a scout like Lily was. But if you don't fancy waiting for that, you could send some pictures to a modelling agency (let your parents know first, though). All they'll want are some good clear snapshots to check if you're photogenic. Don't pay for anything more professional. Turn up to an agency audition wearing smart/casual well-groomed clothes, no make-up and with natural, fresh-washed hair.

You don't have to be conventionally gorgeous. They're out to find the face of tomorrow and that can be quite quirky. You can be plain and get work, and even ugly (see *www.ugly.org*). The Association of Model Agents on 020 7584 6466 will advise on reputable model agencies.

Dancing

BANK ON HIM

Jamie Bell: The teenager who proved that dancing wasn't just for girls. He started taking ballet lessons at 6 before finding film fame as a 14-year-old in the blockbuster *Billy Elliot*.

It's a hard life being a dancer. Whether you want to become a ballerina, like Darcey Bussell, or simply wiggle your hips in music videos, some kind of training, probably at a dance school, is vital. There's a great website dedicated to teens who want to dance. See *www.young-dancers.org* Try also the Royal Ballet School (*www.royal-ballet-school.org.uk*) and the Imperial Society of Teachers of Dancing (*www.istd.org*).

Comedy

BANK ON HER

Susan Nickson: started writing the comedy show *Two Pints of Lager and a Packet of Crisps* when she was still a teenager. She won a short film award when she was 14 and had her first TV programme broadcast on Channel 4 aged 17!

Always making your mates laugh? Bad news is, there's no obvious way to become a comic at a young age. Get involved in theatre and college revues and look for open mic events where you can show off your stand-up routine. Another way in is to try writing topical gags and sketches for other people's shows. Find out who the producers and script editors are for sketch shows – both on radio and TV – and send them your stuff. Check out the BBC's creativity website aimed at 13- to 19-year-olds: *www.bbc.co.uk/blast*

Whatever your talent, there *is* a place for it. Think of Simon Cowell's show *Britain's Got Talent*. Maybe you won't make loads of money out of it, but all sorts of people have ended up in the limelight.

BANK ON THIS

Three Unusual Ways to Showbiz Fame

Nick Park: He was a kid who loved drawing cartoons and made his first animated puppets in his parents' attic at 13. He went on to make plasticine models for TV and ended up as a multi Oscar winner with creations like Wallace and Gromit.

David Blaine: He's the magician who's made a living out of stunts like sitting in a perspex box for 44 days. He started doing magic tricks as a 4-year-old and did street magic before he walked into a TV office in New York and did card tricks and illusions for the company's executives in their boardroom. He was awarded with a million-dollar television contract.

Stanley Unwin: He amazed the world by inventing his own language called Unwinese, where he twisted words around. He became a big star on radio, TV and film.

How to Keep Going

One of the key messages from the business tycoons interviewed earlier is that you're more likely to fail before you succeed. So bear in mind these tips if you're going to be a showbiz success.

BRAIN BOX
Top Tips for Boosting Your Talent

★ **Keep practising:** Whatever your talent, you can always learn more and get better. The better you get the more chances you create.

★ **Keep your options open:** Don't just stick to one thing. If you have several talents, try and keep them all up rather than putting all your eggs in one basket. There's nothing wrong with switching your ambition: look at Billie Piper, who started out as a pop star and became a successful actress.

★ **Take opportunities:** It might not be the one you want, but grab every opportunity: you never know where it might lead.

★ **But be careful:** There are many rip-offs in the entertainment industry and most involve taking money from all the wannabes who don't know any better. Yes, there are talent scouts in the street scouring for the next top model. Yes, there are open auditions for film roles. However, when you see regular ads in the papers looking for the next big thing, you should be wary! Don't pay out to get on the books of an agency or for photos or casting books unless you're sure you're with a reputable agent.

★ **Be professional:** Standards are high out there, so keep an eye on the detail. Scrawled, misspelt notes rarely impress when they arrive as your CV. Turning up late or expecting extensive directions for the route will give the idea you're a lightweight. Forgetting the words of a song or a script will make you seem unprofessional at an audition. Make a checklist for interviews and auditions to ensure everything goes well. Remember: if your dad's satnav goes on the blink, you'll be the one who gets penalized for being late, not him!

★ **Have a fallback option:** Lily Cole knew the importance of getting a good education. The world of showbiz is fickle and it's great to have some qualifications if, one day, you have to end up getting the kind of job that doesn't put your face on the front of lunchboxes.

Max Clifford is the man who 'looks after the stars'. As Britain's leading publicity genius he makes sure people in the limelight don't get into any sticky situations and that they plan their careers properly. Here's his advice.

MAX'S TOP TIPS

What's the best way to get yourself noticed in the entertainment world as a youngster?

If you think you have got a special talent, make yourself known to an agent. The small-time ones are the best to try if you are unknown. They'll know how to get you on TV.

What are the pitfalls to look out for?

Most kids are desperate to be famous. But people can be very jealous if you start to become successful. This means that you have to be prepared for the fact that you won't have many close friends any longer. So you have to be strong. You have to be careful that you don't mind your mum and dad knowing everything about your life too – in case it gets in the newspapers.

How should you use being a teenager to your advantage?

It can be a real advantage to be a star when you're a teenager. For a start, you get the lifestyle – shops will stay open late just so you can visit them. Make·sure you have the right people around you to give you advice, though. That can be the difference between five minutes of fame – and half an hour!

Does it help to be money-minded?

Once you start making a bit of money, make sure you look after it. Believe me, there are a lot of people who have had a lot of money, spent it and now have nothing to show for it. Hang on to some of it in case the fame doesn't last.

What's the best way to not drop out of the limelight?

After you have made that initial breakthrough, make sure you have got someone who can look after you and manage your career. Make sure you pace yourself too. Don't try and do everything at once, otherwise people will, frankly, get sick and tired of your face.

Develop your talent and enjoy it and then, if you do become famous, it will be a bonus.

Let's sum up those ultimate milli-thinking tips for budding talented types who want to get to the top.

★ Don't let shyness or a lack of confidence hold you back.

★ Make sure you love what you do and work on your talent.

★ Everyone involved in the creative arts gets knock-backs. Use them to learn how to give yourself a better shot next time.

★ Be ambitious. But realize that there are thousands trying to do the same. Aim high and concentrate on having fun – that way it won't matter if all your dreams don't come true.

Remember this famous quote about the sometimes fleeting nature of fame and you can't go far wrong . . .

MILLI-MOUTH

'In the future everyone will be famous for fifteen minutes.**'** –
Artist Andy Warhol

Can't sing, act, dance or write? Maybe your talent is more physical?
Up next, sport!

6.
HOW TO BE A SPORT-AIRE

Most of us have dreamed of being a sporting great – whether it's scoring the winning goal in the World Cup or getting a gold medal at the Olympics.

Only a few people get to hit these heights of sporting achievement, but true sporting success is largely measured by the goals you set yourself. And don't believe that old cliché that 'you're just rubbish at sport'. A lot of sporting ability is about practice and confidence as much as natural ability. And while you might not be immediately brilliant at the obvious things, like football or running, there are thousands of different sports – even darts is aiming to be an Olympic discipline!

And don't believe that your physique is a barrier either.

BANK ON THIS
Bodies of Evidence

Ian Thorpe: A chlorine allergy and size 17 feet didn't stop the swimmer becoming World Champion at 15 and bagging a string of Olympic golds.
Shaun Wright-Phillips: At 16 he was told that his frame was too small to make it in football . . . he went on to become the shortest player in the Premiership, at 5ft 5in.

MILLI-MOUTH

❛One of the things that my parents have taught me is never listen to other people's expectations. You should live your own life and live up to your own expectations❜ – *Golfing hero Tiger Woods*

Be a Good Sport

Where do you start if you want to be a sporting success? Get information about sports in your area, even the stuff that doesn't sound up your street. Try clubs or local teams that could be looking for new faces. The other good thing about sport is that it's often free. Shop around before you decide which is best for you. And try to blend natural skills with enjoyment – there aren't many top athletes who hate the sport they're involved in!

Sporting success isn't all about muscles and fitness, though. You have to be dedicated and committed. To be a winner you'll also need to think 'winner'. This is all about developing what athletes call your PMA – positive mental attitude. It's a mind-over-matter thing that takes you from being just good at a sport to becoming truly great. When top athletes are in competition it's usually assumed that all of them are at the peak of their powers. What often makes the difference is the way that they think. Ever see a world-class footballer player about to take a penalty? The net's huge and in training 99 times out of 100 they'd stick it past the keeper. But it isn't such a cinch if you're worried about missing on the big occasion. PMA gives you the confidence to do well, the energy to go that extra mile and helps you use up every inch of your physical capabilities.

BRAIN BOX
Being Positive

★ Talk yourself up. Tell yourself you're good. Muhammad Ali, the boxing superstar, always said, 'I am the greatest'. If you say it enough you'll believe it. Get rid of your negative inner voice. When you talk yourself down or criticize yourself, your body responds to prove you right.

★ Visualize winning. Spend mental rehearsal time sitting with your eyes closed and imagining how it will look, feel and sound when you do well.

★ Don't be too calm. Athletes suffer nerves before an event like anyone else but they use the adrenalin it creates rather than allowing it to use them. Harness all the good effects of being 'jittery', like the way it clears your head and makes you more energetic.

★ Get into the zone. If you watch top athletes just before they compete, they're often staring blankly into space, clearing their mind. It improves performance by enhancing focus and increasing concentration.

★ Take control of your own destiny. Success is in your hands, not anyone else's. The only person who can beat you is a better athlete.

★ Negative thinking blames other people (like trainers, parents) or circumstances (poor equipment, footwear) for any problems.

Believe in yourself and who knows where you might end up.

BANK ON THIS

Three Sporting Stars Who Made it Big in Their Teens

Theo Walcott: Picked for England's World Cup squad at 17, the football genius had already become the most expensive 16-year-old in the history of British football when he was bought by high-flying Premiership side Arsenal.

Maria Sharapova: The Russian tennis player became the third-youngest Wimbledon women's champion in 2004, aged 17. At the end of 2006 she was the world's highest-paid female athlete.

Bobby Fischer: He was only 13 when he became the youngest player ever to win the US Junior Chess Championship. Two years later he was an international grandmaster.

Here's a boxing star who oozes positive mental attitude.

HOT SEAT:
AMIR KHAN

Fast facts

Who: *This wonder kid won a silver medal, as a 17-year-old, at the Athens Olympics in 2004.*

Worth: *Got a £1-million-plus contract when he turned professional at 18. He has already written his autobiography and got a multi-million-pound sponsorship deal with Reebok.*

Trivia bite: *Plans to be world champion by the time he's 21 and reward himself with a Porsche 911.*

Did you always want to be a boxer?

I wanted to be a boxer from the age of 7 or 8 after seeing Muhammad Ali versus George Foreman and getting Muhammad Ali's boxing videos. He always looked great and had loads of people shouting for him.

Where did you get your inspiration?

My inspiration was from watching Muhammad Ali: how he boxed, how he communicated with people and the way people followed him. Also support and encouragement from my teachers was great. When I'd win a contest they would praise me and show off my trophy in the school assembly.

When did you know you had hit the big time?

When I came back from the Olympics with the silver medal the reception I received was overwhelming and amazing. Then, in the morning, seeing the press outside the house asking for pictures and interviews.

Did you have to be fearless, even cocky at times, to get where you are today?

You need to be positive and very confident, but also show respect and not be arrogant.

Have you ever found your age a problem in terms of being taken seriously?

No, not at all. I always achieved what I aimed for and want to continue like that.

What luxury do you spoil yourself with?

I've always believed that if you work hard or train hard and achieve your goals, why not treat yourself? What I'm passionate about are cars and watches.

What ambitions do you have left?

To become a world champion.

What would you say is the secret of your success and what is the biggest risk?

Success is something you have to work hard to achieve. I train, and stay focused, and the biggest risk is losing that focus.

How do you stop it all going to your head?

I have a great family around me and friends looking after me, so if I step out of line or get big-headed they're always there to remind me to keep my feet on the ground.

What music do you listen to?

Mainly hip hop, R and B, dance – as long as it's got a good beat to it.

AMIR'S TOP TIPS

★ Train hard.
★ Stay focused.
★ Be nice.

Spot Your Sport

Try as many different sports as you can to see what you're good at. Remember that there are different types of sporting ability.

You might be good at hand to eye co-ordination, so choose a ball game like tennis or cricket, or you might want to be a motor-racing driver. Maybe your sporting ability relies on strength and combat skills, so karate or rugby might be the right thing for you. What about stamina? Maybe you've got real powers of endurance, so long-distance running or battling the elements on a boat could be the right avenue. Or maybe it's not your body but your brain that's your biggest asset: think of games like chess.

However, you'll probably be good at more than one sport. Practise a couple before making a decision. Many sports stars hedged their bets before concentrating on one type of sport in which to really make their mark.

BANK ON THIS

One Star Who Changed His Sport

Ian Botham: Probably England's most famous-ever cricketer, he played football for Scunthorpe United before turning to cricket.

You also need to work out if you prefer being a team player or going solo.

BANK ON THIS

Teen Who Did It Solo

Michael Perham: At the age of 14 he became the youngest person to sail the Atlantic Ocean single-handedly in a nine-metre yacht called *Cheeky Monkey*.

MILLI-FACT

Fishing is often said to be Britain's most popular sport, with ten million people regularly involved.

Whichever sport you decide to aim for, all of them will have one thing in common: to be the best you're going to have to practise – hard.

How to Practise and Train

Hard work and dedication isn't something you read or see a lot of in sport. Why? Because it's attractive to think our heroes have some magical power and don't need all the hard slog of practice sessions.

The truth is, all great sports people put in hours of graft. It might look like they spend most of their life clubbing, posing for pictures or down at the tattoo parlour, but that's only because the cameras aren't so interested in showing the unexciting dedication behind all the magic.

Huge amounts of flair will only get you so far, and everyone has periods where their natural talent will not be firing on all cylinders. Putting some 'grit' into your game will help improve that performance. Here's a guide to help get it.

BRAIN BOX

Succeed at Practice and Training

★ Think of each match or competition as the very small tip of a very large iceberg. Hours, days, weeks and years of hard work are needed to get you to this one peak.

★ Be dedicated. Take what you do seriously, even if you're not winning all the time.

★ Be committed. Work your skills all the time.

★ Inspire yourself. Watch your heroes play or compete. Get their autobiographies and read up on their lives and what inspired them.

★ Make your sport a lifestyle thing. Being fit means healthy eating and masses of sleep and fresh air.

★ Make your training sessions non-negotiable. We only quit when our brain starts to make excuses. If you go to bed thinking that you'll go to train if you can get up early enough, your brain will hear that as a 'don't bother'. The minute you start to create alternatives like late nights or 'if I feel like it', you're starting to quit. Know your most dangerous 'quit' points, like early mornings or when it's freezing cold. Stick inspirational notes around your bed before you go to sleep to motivate yourself as soon as you wake up.

★ Pick some music and load it on to a tape or download to your iPod. With your favourite tunes blasting in your ears you're unlikely to lack enthusiasm or energy.

MILLI-MOUTH

❝The harder I practise, the luckier I get!❞ – *Golfing star Gary Player*

Coming up next is one top football manager who reckons practice is the key for any wannabe soccer star.

HOT SEAT:
HARRY REDKNAPP

Fast facts

Who: *Coach who has managed clubs like West Ham, Southampton and Portsmouth.*

Success factor: *Successful player turned manager, taking Portsmouth to the dizzy heights of the Premiership.*

Trivia bite: *He's helped a few young people shine in his time – not least his own son Jamie, who became a Premiership player and married pop star Louise.*

What's your biggest tip for budding footballers?

Don't worry too much about whether you have got talent or not – that's for other people to decide really. The most important thing is to practise, practise and practise. The more time you spend with a football the better. I remember seeing Frank Lampard still practising at training two hours after everyone else had gone home.

What is the best way to get your skills noticed?

Get into as many teams as you can – the school team first of all, then a youth team and maybe a county team. Don't worry about approaching the clubs direct. These days there are loads of talent scouts out there. If you're good enough they'll find you. Keep going. Listen to, and learn from, people who know about the game.

What are the main dangers?

Make sure you carry on with your studies for as long as possible – in case football doesn't work out. As I said, you need to practise but don't let the pressure become too much. You should be enjoying playing the game – that's the main thing and your parents need to understand this too.

How do you make sure you stay in shape?

The most successful footballers tend to look after themselves and avoid distractions that come with the lifestyle. It's only one or two that let it go to their heads. Make sure you watch your diet and eat healthy food.

And if it doesn't seem to be going too well?

If you want it badly enough, then just go for it. Lots of players have been dropped by one club and taken up by another and still succeeded. Being a professional footballer is a good career and you can make a lot of money. Good luck to those that do – after all, it can be a short career.

MILLI-FACT

While the top players rake in eye-spinning incomes, it's not like that for most hard-working professional players. The average one in League Two earns £49,600 a year.

Next up is the original 'Boy Wonder', a sporting superstar who hit the big time while still in his teens. Unlike some other stars, he kept his focus on football, rather than on some of the other distractions on offer.

HOT SEAT:
RYAN GIGGS

Fast facts

Who: *The wonder winger and Manchester United star.*

Success factor: *Spotted playing football in the streets at 14 by Manchester City scouts, he ended up going professional for Alex Ferguson at 17 and making his league debut a year later. He's helped Manchester United to win all the top titles.*

Trivia bite: *Giggs has scored 11 goals for the Welsh national side.*

When did you know you wanted to be a professional footballer?

When I was at school I wanted to play rugby league, but then started playing soccer and I enjoyed running past the other players. It was when playing for a Sunday league team I knew that soccer was for me.

What was difficult about being successful so young?

It did not affect me too much. I was concentrating on training and being a good player. The press was the worst, trying to get interviews. That was when I realized I needed an agent.

Describe how it felt when you first scored for Manchester United?

This will always be in my memory. It was my full debut against Manchester City on 4 May 1991, at home. I didn't even know I was playing until the boss came in and said, 'You're playing on the left.' I scored the only goal.

Once you were earning a good wage, did you celebrate?
No. Playing is not about the money; it's the team that comes first and winning, and after you have won you can celebrate. That's the important thing – winning.

What was your biggest setback and how did you deal with it?
I had many setbacks. When you get injured your head drops, you hate every minute, especially on match days. It makes you spend every moment getting back to match fitness.

Do you like being famous?
I don't think of myself as being famous. I am an ordinary person doing a job he enjoys, who plays for a famous football club.

What would be your perfect Christmas present?
Good health for my family and friends.

Do you have a favourite gadget?
With two children I don't have time for gadgets.

MILLI-FACT
Trevor Francis became the first player bought by a football club, Nottingham Forest, for £1 million, back in 1979.

How to Lose Without Being a Loser

What's the difference between someone who loses at sport and someone who is a sport loser? Losing at sport is part of the package if you're going to become a winner, but only if you take it in the right way.

BRAIN BOX
Lose It, Then Use It

★ Losing is a vital part of learning how to win.

★ Be a good loser. It's good to be passionate about your sport, but don't turn that passion into useless anger if you get beaten.

★ Don't blame other people for losing. When you do this you fail to spot valuable lessons in your own behaviour.

★ Don't give up.

★ Work out what went wrong so that you don't repeat any mistakes. Always use a loss to improve your own performance.

★ If you keep losing you'll have to make a change. Saying 'I can only do my best' might not work. If you always do what you've always done, you'll always get what you always got. Instead of playing the same way, try making small changes just to see what effect they have. Sometimes a tiny change of tactic can have a very big impact on your game. Doing something differently can rev your brain up and refresh it, or make you see things in a different way. Some sports people change boots or bats or racquets. Some boxers even switch which hand they lead with during a bout just to confuse their opponent.

★ Allow a short time to be angry or fed up about losing – after all it's only natural – but make sure you don't stay down. Move on – but in an upwards direction.

★ When others beat you, they provide you with clues about how to beat them the next time.

To win at sport you need to be passionate and dedicated, which means managing some very strong emotions. When you're playing at high levels, it's what's in your head that can scupper your performance.

BRAIN BOX

How to Manage Your Emotions

★ Control your anger. We've all seen sporting types lose it and we've all seen them suffer the consequences. It either puts them off their game or it gets them thrown off.

★ Keep a cool, analytical mind whenever the going gets tough. Do this by staying focused.

★ By keeping your temper you're keeping control of yourself. This makes you very powerful. By comparison, getting mad only makes you look tough for a nanosecond.

★ If you start to lose it, think of a role model. Imagine you're them until the moment passes. You need to burn your emotions as extra fuel and energy for your sport. Think of emotions as fuel, not something that sits in the driving seat!

★ Try a couple of simple mantras: 'Save it' is a good one to put a lid on your feelings. Breathe out. Emotions settle around the lower lung and stomach. By breathing out air you release all that pent-up anger.

Breaking the Rules

When it comes to who should do what in sport, there are no cast-iron rules. Boys don't have to be Vinnie Jones-style hard men and girls don't have to stick to netball.

Don't shy away from activities that might not seem to offer sporting glory. Everything from judo to curling and skateboarding to extreme ironing (yes, it does exist) could be the ticket to stardom and success.

Here's a star who broke with traditional sporting stereotypes.

HOT SEAT:
ISA GUHA

Fast facts

Who: *Star of England's women's cricket team.*
Success factor: *By the time she was 17 she was playing for England and has been a regular in the national side ever since.*
Trivia bite: *In 2002 Isa won the BBC Asian Sports Personality of the Year award.*

Who or what inspired you to play cricket?

My parents and brother have been a massive influence on my life. Without their support and encouragement I would never be here. The number of miles my father would drive at weekends and my mother during the week just to get me to training or to matches around the country! As parents go, I think they found the right balance between pressuring me and letting me do what I wanted to do. Playing cricket with my brother in the back garden gave me my competitive edge and as a youngster I looked up to him a lot. I have also been very lucky in the teams that I've played in and the people I've met along the way. I have gained a lot of support and inspiration from my friends and people within the game. I owe a lot to them too.

Could you describe your cricketing experiences at school?

I started playing cricket when I was 8, along with other sports. My parents encouraged me to join the local cricket club that my brother was already playing for and I started off with the boys' colts as there weren't any girls' teams. At school I took part in other activities, like hockey and athletics, but I went to an all-girls' grammar school so cricket was not on the agenda. My father set up an all-girls' section at the club and I got into the Thames Valley under-21 team when I was 11. I went to a few regional trials before I got into the England development squad when I was 15. All the while I was playing boys cricket, which was extremely beneficial in the long run. At school I made some great friends, who I still keep in touch with. They keep me grounded, because we hardly talk about the cricket. Growing up I'd want to go out with them on a Friday night but I'd have a match or training the next morning, so it was hard as a teenager from that point of view. I'd have to compromise and get picked up at 11 p.m., but as I got older I realized how important that compromise was.

Do you have any advice for girls going into cricket or sport in general?

Obviously the main thing is that you enjoy what you are doing and are not pressured into anything. One thing I think is very important is to have other activities to focus on, because it is very easy to burn out. I played a number of different sports until I was 16 and still play badminton when I can. Not only did it help with becoming more all-rounded with my skills, but it gave me a release from playing cricket day in day out. I would also like to emphasize that it is OK to play sport at the highest level, study and maintain a decent social life if you put your mind to it.

What did it feel like playing for England for the first time?

I was 17 when I played my first game for England. It was a whirlwind experience as I had been drafted into the squad at short notice. I found out the night before that I was playing the opening game against India in the 2002 Tri series. I wasn't expecting to open the bowling but Connie (Clare Connor, ex-England captain) came over to me during warm-ups to say that I would be given the new ball. Obviously I was ecstatic, but the nerves grew stronger . . . I had a lot of support from the girls, who were a lot older than me at the time. I just went out there and played the way I normally play. There is nothing that can describe the feeling you get when you pull on an England shirt . . . I have an enormous sense of pride every time I walk on to the pitch.

Do you have other career ambitions? Can you make a living in women's cricket?

Unfortunately women's cricket is semi-professional so it is hard to make a living by just playing cricket. We have lottery funding from Sport England, so 24 players in the country get a sum of money each month which is spent on training and travel costs. Half of them get a contribution towards living expenses. Most of the girls have part-time jobs with understanding employers that allow them to go on tour. I am currently in my final year studying for a BSc in biochemistry at University College London. Scientific research is something that really interests me. If I can get a 2.1 degree this year then I plan to do a PhD. However, playing cricket is always part of my long-term plan.

Have you had to overcome any setbacks?

I haven't had any major setbacks from a personal point of view. Obviously I can find it hard every now and then to juggle all of my commitments and I am prone to burn out, but with such a great support system I am motivated to do well and succeed. I was guilty of a fairy-tale beginning and then realized that you need to work extremely hard if you want to stay at the top. The game has become a lot more competitive, so I am always making sure I stay one step ahead.

ISA'S TOP TIPS

To achieve the best you must have:
- ★ A passion for what you do.
- ★ A good attitude.
- ★ A hard-work ethic and discipline.
- ★ Open-mindedness to criticism, as it will make you a better player.

It's always wise to keep your options open as long as you can. Even the most talented athletes can have setbacks, like injuries, which mean they must consider alternative careers. Here we talk to a pair of sporting twins who have stayed positive despite setbacks.

HOT SEAT:
BRYONY AND KATHRYN FROST

Fast facts

Who: *Steeple-chasers who are hot favourites for the 2012 Olympics.*

Success factor: *As teens in 2003 they were rated as numbers one and two UK juniors in their sport and picked up big advertising deals with Adidas and Lucozade.*

Trivia bite: *Turned down modelling offers to concentrate on training and study.*

Why did you both decide to concentrate on athletics?
Bryony and Kathryn: From a young age we realized we had a talent at running. Being twins we always had that extra competitive spirit between us and often found ourselves racing each other whenever we saw an open space! We adored the feeling of sprinting our hearts

out on the beach or in the countryside where we lived on the Isle of Wight. We were about 10 years old when we told our mum our ambition was to be in the Olympics!

When did you realize just how good you were?

Bryony: We easily won our local races – be it at the Brownies or school sports day – and we quickly gained a reputation as 'the running twins'. When we were young we never took it seriously and didn't do any training. Despite this, we were faster than all the other girls who regularly went down to the athletics track. Eventually an athletics coach, Geoff Watkins, spotted us and suggested we came down and joined in the training sessions. Once we'd joined the club, and with the inspiration we gained from meeting Geoff, we quickly went from being local heroes to being international athletes.

You must have met some famous people in your time. Who were you inspired by?

Bryony: Not particularly. We kept ourselves away from the celebrity lifestyle at Loughborough University and concentrated on training. However I was awestruck when meeting Paula Radcliffe, who lives and trains at Loughborough, as she was such an inspiration to me. She's great and really down to earth and will always spend time to chat to all the athletes.

Have you had to give things up to put in the hours training?

Bryony: Of course you compromise a lot to be able to train to the highest level. I didn't have a lot of time for other hobbies. Boyfriends had to be understanding and have been generally athletically minded themselves. We really had to work hard to balance our degree and training and had to become a bit of a recluse at times!

Kathryn: We have done athletics all our lives, so we never knew any different and therefore we never felt like we gave anything up.

However, we certainly didn't live a typical teenager's life. Our lives were dominated by our ambition to be great athletes.

You used the money you made to put yourselves through college while you were training. Is it important for teenagers to be money savvy as well as have talent?

Bryony and Kathryn: We used our money to help us with training and college, which wasn't easy at times. It can be really tough for teenagers at university. Many students are used to living with parents that pay for all their food and living costs. They soon have to learn how to budget and get themselves through university. All students are notoriously tight with money but most still have to rely on help from parents. It got particularly tight for us in our final year and we would dread it when the landlord asked for the month's rent. Luckily we had supportive parents. However, you have to accept that debt will be inevitable. It is a real concern when you finish university and have not secured full-time employment. Then you are in the real world!

You once said you love to go shopping. What little luxuries do you like treating yourself to?

Bryony: I have to say we are very careful with our money. We are both living London, which makes budgeting more difficult. I do, however, love to treat myself to nice meals out with friends. I love Primark, which means I can treat myself to new clothes without racking up a large bill!

Are you still aiming to compete at the 2012 Olympics? What are your future ambitions?

Bryony: Unfortunately Kathryn and I have had real injury problems in the last few years. Both of us trained hard at a young age, below a healthy weight. This has really taken its toll on our bodies and we both suffer from a low bone density in our lower spine, with Kathryn being diagnosed with osteoporosis. Obviously our priorities have changed to getting healthy for the time being and we have had to cut down our training and tried to put on weight, which has not been easy. We hope that our bodies will be able to cope with top-class athletic training again and we will be able to compete. However, we are taking it one step at a time at the moment and we cannot rush the recovery process. We were both able to study bone density in our final-year dissertation at Loughborough University and are aware of what needs to be done to help us achieve a healthier body. Anorexia and eating disorders are so common in female athletes and I don't think the long-term consequences are fully understood and addressed. Perhaps success at a young age should be compromised in favour of a healthy body and more chance of a sustained and successful career in athletics.

BRYONY AND KATHRYN'S TOP TIPS

★ Enjoy how athletics makes you feel and enjoy the social side of it. You will have many great experiences that will stay with you throughout life.

★ Don't put pressure on yourself to be a great junior athlete. If you stick at it you can be a great senior, but don't expect it to happen straight away. Doing too much too soon can lead to injury and early retirement.

★ Have a goal. This needs to be personal to you and achievable. Once you have achieved it, set another. This will give you the feeling that you are moving forward and progressing in a positive way. It also keeps you focused and determined and gives you a great sense of achievement.

Get a Kick Start

Some schools are good for sport, but if you want to play on the big stage you need to go beyond what they have to offer. This lot can help take your sporting ambition ★ the next level.

BANK ON THIS
On Your Marks

Tennis: It used to have a reputation for being a posh sport, but fiery Scot Andy Murray has changed all that. The Lawn Tennis Association has junior tennis academies, see *www.lta.org.uk* Also look out for schemes like Ariel's tennis competitions for young people. See *www.ariel.co.uk/ariel_tennis.html*

Football: The Football Association's website is a great place to start and can advise on local youth clubs, academies, diets and choosing the right boots: *www.thefa.com*

Golf: The English Golf Union has a special section on tips and youth competitions. See *www.englishgolfunion.org*

Athletics: UK Athletics has teamed up with Norwich Union to help 8- to 15-year-olds improve their skills. See *www.ukathletics.net* that also has a list of local athletics clubs.

Cricket: The English Cricket Board has set up a site to help you find your local club: *www.play-cricket.com* Check out their main website for more info on Kwik Cricket and Urban cricket too: *www.ecb.co.uk*

Motor sports: You can get started as young as 8. Go to the Getting Started section on the Motor Sports Association website: *www.msauk.org*

Boxing: You can find a local club through the Amateur Boxing Association. See *www.abae.co.uk*

Disability sport: Check out these websites: *www.efds.net* and *www.paralympics.org.uk*

Also look out for sporting scholarships and visit the websites of the Youth Sport Trust (*www.youthsporttrust.org*) and Sport England (*www.sportengland.org*) for more links and info on how to take your sport to the max, from rugby to rowing.

Make the Most of It

Aaron Lennon is a young star and top footballer for England. He reckons it's important to enjoy your talent. After all, it won't last forever and by making fun your priority you won't go far wrong.

HOT SEAT:
AARON LENNON

Fast facts

Who: *Football ace famous for his lightning speed.*

Success factor: *This wonder winger went to the Leeds United football academy before becoming the youngest player ever to appear in the FA Premier League at the age of 16 years and 129 days. He has since made a transfer to Tottenham and was one of England's best players in the 2006 World Cup.*

Trivia bite: *England manager Steve McLaren on Aaron's speed: 'I remember on the first day of training everyone took a step back and went "phew".'*

Why did you choose a career in football?

My older brother, Anthony, was always a very good footballer and he used to let me play with him and his mates. I was comparatively small but had to keep up. It taught me that it doesn't matter how disadvantaged you are, if you try hard enough you can succeed.

Is it possible to make it in football if you aren't loud or aggressive?

I'm not very vocal myself, but you just have to look at the likes of Sol Campbell or Ryan Giggs to realize that it is what you do with the ball that counts.

How do you spoil yourself now that you have made it big?

I have just bought a dream house so that all my family can come and visit. They are all in Leeds and because I don't get a break at Christmas, they can all come and do dinner at my place now!

What is the best thing about playing for England?
Two things: the opportunity to play with and against the world's elite, but also just fulfilling the childhood dream of representing my country in the World Cup.

What tips would you give someone who wants to make it in football?
Don't drink, smoke or take your health for granted. Work hard, never give up faith in your dreams, and be grateful for every opportunity you get.

How should young people avoid getting into problems?
The greatest pitfall is that you can lose everything in a fraction of a second through injury. Therefore, while you should enjoy every second of your life as a footballer, you must always remember how lucky you are and that in football, and life in general, others aren't so fortunate.

Finally, to get yourself into the sporting mindset, ponder this thought from a sporting legend.

MILLI-MOUTH
❮One chance is all you need.❯ –
American running legend, Jesse Owens

7.
HOW TO BE A WEB-ILLIONAIRE

The Internet is probably the most exciting creative tool of our age. And while your mum, dad or teacher might struggle to get to grips with them, computers and their gadgets and games, and the world of the web are transforming everybody's lives, with new inventions and ideas happening all the time. With age on your side, you're perfectly poised to be part of the on-going technological revolution.

Some people feel that they're being left behind with every new computer craze or console that comes along. But developing your online skills and getting computer savvy could help open up a huge range of opportunities. Whether it's setting up websites, creating businesses online or designing games or gadgets, the possibilities are endless.

This chapter will tell you how to start looking at your computer, the web and games not only as things that are 'just there' but as things that are almost alive, growing and developing in front of your eyes. They are tools that you can use in your own personal journey into the future. As well as picking up some inspirational thoughts from people who have made use of them, we'll give you top tips on how to get your mind to compute the right net knowledge.

MILLI-MOUTH

❝I have been quoted saying that, in the future, all companies will be Internet companies. I still believe that.❞ – *Andrew Grove, Intel computer tycoon*

The best news is that you don't need much to get a computer- or gadget-based idea off the ground. If you have access to a computer at home or at school, you don't need vast amounts of money to get going. If you're starting a business, your customers or target audience could be there at the touch of a keyboard and if it's a new piece of kit or, say, a game idea, then the people who can help will almost certainly understand where you're coming from because they'll share your passion for new ideas.

BANK ON THIS

Two Young Techno Success Stories

Alex Tew: He is the student who set up *www.milliondollarhomepage.com* to raise money to get himself through university. The idea came from a brainstorming session where he wrote on a pad: 'How can I become a millionaire?' Twenty minutes later he had come up with the idea to sell a page worth of pixels – the dots which make up a computer screen – as advertising space for companies. Each pixel cost a dollar. In just over a year he had made his target of $1 million.

Tom Hadfield: He founded Soccernet, a sports Internet company, aged 13 from his bedroom. In 1999, while he was studying for his GCSEs, he sold it for £25 million.

Spin Your Own Web

There are different kinds of Internet-based businesses. Here are some of them.

Sharing Stuff

Sites that allow people to keep in touch and share content are called social networking websites. Examples include *www.friendsreunited.co.uk*, *www.facebook.com*, *www.MySpace.com* and *www.youtube.com*

BANK ON THIS

Video kings: Friends Chad Hurley and Steve Chen set up the video-sharing site YouTube from a garage in 2005. It was recently bought by Google for over £800 million.

Facebooker prize: At 22 years old Mark Zuckerberg turned down a $1 billion offer for his website, Facebook, which started as a tool for university students to keep in touch and has since become the seventh busiest site on the Internet.

Searching for Stuff

Search engines like Yahoo and Google started by helping people to get round the Internet. Some have expanded into huge money-making machines offering services from advertising to maps.

BANK ON THIS

Google giants: Larry Page fell in love with computers when he was 6. In his twenties he and friend Sergey Brin had the idea to set up a search engine that ranked websites by popularity. Their company has since been floated on the stock market and is worth billions.

Selling and Buying Stuff

Think of auction sites like eBay, comparison websites like *www.kelkoo.co.uk* and sites that specialize in selling things like *www.amazon.co.uk*

BANK ON THIS

eBay wonder: Pierre Omidyar was 28 when he sat down over a weekend back in the 1990s to write the program that was to become eBay. His personal wealth is now estimated in the billions.

The services you can provide on the Internet are probably infinite and also include things like Internet security, dating, providing email, and information sites, like Wikipedia or the BBC.

Here's a truly web-rilliant woman who founded one of the world's most iconic and successful sites . . .

HOT SEAT:
MARTHA LANE FOX

Fast facts.

Who: *The co-founder of lastminute.com, which revolutionized the travel industry.*

Success factor: *Founded lastminute.com in 1998 with pal Brent Hoberman. It went on to be worth millions. She's now left the company and started a new karaoke business called Lucky Voice.*

Trivia bite: *She spent a year recovering in hospital after a horrible car crash on holiday in Morocco.*

When did you first decide you wanted to be a businesswoman?

I never really decided upon business; I always liked new ideas and the challenge of making them happen.

Is it wrong to believe that boys are more into computers and new technologies than girls?

Traditionally I think boys were pushed towards technology, but this is starting to change with new technology like the web and iPods.

As a teenage girl, were you encouraged to think women could make it in business? What could have been better in schools?

Luckily I went to mixed schools where we were always treated equally and made to feel we could do anything. I'm sure my experience was unusual and that more schools could definitely build women's confidence around issues of leadership, management and innovation.

What was the secret of *lastminute.com*?

There's no single secret, I'm afraid. It was a combination of things, starting with the brilliance of my business partner Brent's original idea, but I think a great team, a lot of energy and determination certainly helped us.

You achieved a lot of fame with *lastminute.com*. What was the best thing about being a big success?

The best things were the access to meeting new people and the possibility of travelling, which I love.

What was the biggest challenge running such an outstanding firm so young?

Finding the right balance between developing new and exciting aspects of the business at the same time as relentlessly concentrating on the core proposition. Also making sure you are constantly recruiting fabulous people to work alongside you.

Did your accident make you even more determined in business?

The accident has made me more determined to do something valuable with my life. It doesn't necessarily have to be a commercial role.

How do you spoil yourself?

I buy far too many things online. There are endless packages arriving at my house every day!

What ambitions do you have left?

With Nick Thistleton, the managing director of Lucky Voice, I would like to bring singing to more of the population. I would also be keen to develop my charitable interests.

What was your favourite hobby as a youngster?

My favourite hobby was writing plays with all the main parts for myself and then I made my brother play just a small minor role!

MARTHA'S TOP TIPS

★ Focus on new technology and what you are offering your customer.

★ Raise as much money as you can to give the business a safe base.

★ Get the best people around you to help you develop the business quickly.

OK, so you're a net nut, but how do you start thinking like a dotcom business person?

BRAIN BOX

How to Get Computerized Thinking

Whether you're a full-on computer geek or just a web-surfing fan, you can use your computer talents to do something fab. You don't need to be a genius or even have advanced knowledge of the Internet. These tips will help you get in the right frame of mind to turn technology to your advantage.

★ Dotcom-ers have the ability to think laterally.

★ Lateral thinking means looking at things in a different way. For instance, cleaning your teeth. How do you do it at the moment? How many other ways could you do it? You know it's good to brush your teeth and you know why it's good but imagine you were trying to invent an alternative. Try to think as creatively and differently as possible. What if you stopped tooth-brushing altogether? What if you worked on removable teeth or replaceable teeth? What about self-cleaning teeth, like a self-cleaning oven? What if you invented food that cleans teeth as you eat? Or food that doesn't need teeth? What about invisible tooth and gum protectors?

★ Most brilliant dotcom ideas come under the 'Why didn't I think of that?' category. People invent sites that are simple but compulsive. You don't need to be an intellectual giant, just have a way of seeing what people (like you!) want.

★ Think about what works and why it works. For example, people like to learn quirky or basic things quickly. *Videojug.com* specializes in short films that teach you almost everything, from kissing to folding a shirt. It's easy but only if you think slightly differently.

★ Write a list of all the things you enjoy doing on the Internet. Then look at the gaps, rather than what's on the list. What would you like to do but can't? What hasn't been done yet but needs to be?

★ Write an 'explosion' of ideas, ranging from the wildest to the most ridiculous to the most ordinary. Let your brain really go on this one. Don't police it with thoughts like 'silly', 'no-brainer' or 'it would never work'. To come up with one great idea you're going to sift through a whole load that won't work too.

★ Spend spare time exercising your lateral thinking by questioning everything you do. Buy a book of lateral-thinking puzzles. There are loads on the market and they'll exercise your lateral-thinking brain muscles.

Building Your Net Biz

All of the usual business rules already covered in this book still apply, but here are some other big issues to think about if you're going to build a successful Internet business.

What Kind of Site?

It may be best to stick to a subject you already know something about. You should certainly start by getting on a search engine and finding out who else might be doing something similar and how they're doing it. Ask yourself if there is something the other sites don't do or that you could do better.

Setting It Up

You'll need to think about getting a good, catchy 'domain name' and web hosting for your site. This need not cost a lot, but think about who will design your site. You can buy ready-made business site packages – or do you fancy learning how to do it using a software package? How will the design help you attract and keep customers/visitors? Also consider how to get your site ranked high up on the search engines or no one will ever find it. If you're thinking of using the net to sell stuff, you might consider starting out by using someone else's site. Lots of people have started successful businesses using auction sites like eBay.

MILLI-FACT

The average time spent by an Internet user on a web page is 48 seconds.

How Will It Make Money?

Will your site make cash through people subscribing (paying to sign up) to your content because it's so useful? Maybe it will be such a clever idea that companies will want to pay you to advertise on your web space. Or are you going to be selling something through the site? In which case you need to consider how people place orders, how you will take orders, how you will get stuff to them and make sure you comply with all the government regulations about selling stuff on the net too.

BANK ON THIS

Teenager Adam Beasant has come up with a novel way of making a million – by trying to build the world's longest list of names and charging people a tiny amount each to have theirs added. See *www.theworldslongestlist.com*

Running the Website

You'll have to make sure that the content is up to date and be able to deal with people's enquiries. It's a good idea not to make the site too complicated at first – slowly build up what you offer. Think about your customer too. Is this something your grandparents could use or are you going for a niche market? Do you want to do all that day-to-day technical stuff, or is someone else going to take care of that side of things?

More Info

For a step-by-step guide to setting up a web-based business, see *www.businesslink.gov.uk*

Next is a millionaire Internet entrepreneur who set up a site to buy cool things – and made it happen with very little money.

HOT SEAT:
MICHAEL SMITH

Fast facts

Who: *Millionaire founder of gadget and gizmo website* www.firebox.com

Success factor: *Set it up with a friend from college and turned it into a company that is worth around £10 million.*

Trivia bite: *Started with £1,000 borrowed from parents.*

Did you always dream of being an entrepreneur?

Yes! I was always driving my family crazy with half-brained ideas as a kid (chicken farms, designing a computer-games magazine, BMX stunt shows, etc.). I then graduated on to running a betting ring, age 12, at school (until I got caught!).

Where did you first get the idea for Firebox? Did you always like boys' toys yourselves?

I've always loved games and gadgets. If I wasn't running Firebox I'd probably be its biggest customer – it's a dream job. Tom (the guy I set up Firebox with) and I wanted to set up a business when we left uni, but had no idea in what area. I thought the smartest idea would be to do something we personally liked so it wouldn't seem like a job. The happiest people in life are those whose work and play are one and the same.

I believe your parents helped you to finance Firebox. But what special challenges did you face as a young person trying to set up a business?

Yes, my parents gave me £1,000 to get started. Everyone was surprisingly helpful, which was great. We didn't have a clue what we were doing but people we spoke to (local 'business link', HSBC bank, other entrepreneurs, etc.) were hugely supportive.

What dangers would you tell teens to watch out for?
Get as much advice for free as you can. Be very nervous if someone asks you to pay for their advice when you are just setting up. Also, don't listen to all the naysayers. You'll meet lots of people who will think your idea is crazy and too risky. If you feel passionate about it, just go for it.

You have said you still travel to work on the bus, but as a millionaire what little luxuries do you have?
I love video games, so I own more consoles than I have space for – a PS1, PS2, Xbox 360, Nintendo DS, Nintendo Wii, and PSP. I just bought a 42-inch HD TV that is probably my most extravagant luxury. I'm thinking of buying a house-boat, so that's probably where I'll end up sinking the rest of my money!

What's the secret of turning a great idea into reality?
Do your research, read as much about the subject as you, speak to experts, and then – just go for it. Too many people have great ideas but they never end up actually starting and making it happen.

Where do you get your ideas?
I read as much as I can. It's very useful for sparking off new ideas: blogs, magazines, autobiographies of entrepreneurs, business books, newspapers. Inspiration also comes from meeting lots of people from different walks of life. I try to attend lots of parties and events in as many related fields as possible.

What's your favourite gadget and why?
Tough question – there are so many to choose from. I think at the moment it would have to be my blue LED binary watch.

MICHAEL'S TOP TIPS

★ Make the site as simple to use as possible (for example, *flickr.com*, *moo.com*).

★ Create a site or product that people will want to talk about and share with their friends. It's possible to build huge, global brands these days purely through word-of-mouth.

★ Empower your users – put them in charge. Give them the tools to create their own content. It can be a lot more powerful than trying to manage everything through a top–down approach (for example, *etsy.com*, *digg.com*, *facebook.com*).

Game On

Does this sound like you: 'It's difficult to think of an Internet business – I just love playing games on my computer and console?' Well, you could turn your love of games into a business. Some gamers have even made their fortunes by turning professional.

MILLI-FACT

Johnathan Wendel is the world's most successful video gamer. He has made over £160,000 in competitions, mainly in what's called the CyberAthlete Professional League.

And we spoke to another gamer who turned his hobby into a living.

HOT SEAT:
RUPERT LOMAN

Fast facts
Who: *Boss of online gaming site Eurogamer.*
Success factor: *Set it up at school when he was 16 and has turned it into a million-pound business. See www.eurogamer.net and www.eurogamer.tv*
Trivia bite: *Runs the company with his brother Nick.*

When did you first become interested in gaming? Did your hobby become your business?

I've been into computer games most of my life, but it was during high school that I became a 'hardcore' gamer. I used to play online computer games in 1996/7 a lot (when I was 13/14). Because there wasn't much in the way of organized competition for the hardcore players, I started to run online games leagues and local 'LAN parties' (where people bring their computers together to a venue to play against each other).

This developed into a business in 1999 when my brother and I founded Eurogamer and started organizing events on a larger scale. We also started selling the tournament management software we had created to run our own events. But it only really started to make money in 2001 when I finished my A levels and decided to run the business full time instead of going to university.

When did you realize there was money to be made in online gaming?

It is not something we set out to do to make money – it was just my hobby and my passion. Most of our big breaks have been the result of us doing something cool and new off our own backs (such as the LAN parties ten years ago, or launching the Eurogamer website seven years ago) and sponsors and advertisers getting in touch because they saw the potential and wanted to get involved.

How did you go about starting up your business?

We just got out there and started doing it. We ran events for friends and people we'd met online, which grew through word of mouth. We got on the phone and asked companies for sponsorship. Most importantly, because it was something we loved doing, it didn't feel like a job and it was a couple of years before we realized that what we were doing could be a business.

We were young and had never run a business before, and as a result we made a lot of mistakes and learnt very fast.

Eurogamer now is exclusively a media publishing business. We no longer run events, but we run some of the most popular video-games websites in Europe. We could never have predicted this was how the business would end up, but we are always flexible and can adapt to where the market is going to go.

How were you financed?

We didn't get any outside funding. Instead, at a time when other online gaming companies were spending millions of pounds of investors' money, we operated on the basis that we wouldn't spend money we didn't have. My brother did various programming jobs for other companies to bring in money to pay the staff we had taken on and we did borrow a small amount of money from our parents – which we've now paid back! We didn't pay ourselves a penny for over two years.

How much has the business grown?

The business has grown to the point where we have 16 full-time employees and a turnover of £1 millon a year. And it's growing rapidly!

Are there specific issues involved in setting up an Internet business?

There are a lot of things we thought were unnecessary costs when we were starting up (and it is very important to keep costs down!). Now we realize they may have helped us if we'd embraced them earlier. Even if you are a cutting-edge business, you will still end up dealing with people who are 'old school' and you will need to prove to them that you are credible.

For example, we started the business without an office. We didn't see the point in people all driving to an expensive office to then sit at their computers and email all day. This was great at the beginning, but it presents a communication challenge. We've developed online systems for collaborative working that do work well, but eventually we relented and we now have a core team of sales and technology staff together, which makes communication much easier. However our journalists still work from home, so we haven't completely changed!

How would you advise young people with similar business ideas and what might be the future challenges in this industry?

The big companies have now recognized online gaming and community websites as a huge growth area, and are all investing heavily in creating their own. So we were lucky to be there early enough before everyone else cottoned on.

If you are young and looking to start a business, then you should concentrate on what you know about and enjoy, and try to do something new. Be prepared for a lot of hard work and don't expect to instantly become a millionaire.

I would also recommend avoiding venture capitalists at all costs – at least until you have become successful enough to take on funding completely on your own terms!

And finally, try and involve people you know and trust – particularly family – in your venture. They are the ones who will help you out through thick and thin, and don't be afraid of getting their advice and help. You won't be able to do everything yourself.

What's your favourite computer game of all time?
Quake 2. The best online game ever.

MILLI-FACT

Will Wright, the brains behind The Sims game, where players create their own virtual world, never settled at school and college, but since he found computers in his early twenties he has become a multi-millionaire off the back of his creation.

Watch Out!

Loads of people – including plenty of teens – made fortunes fast with online business ideas. But just as many lost out big time when the dotcom market crashed a few years back. If your business starts growing, be prepared for it falling apart.

Also, make sure that what you are doing online is safe. Tell your parents what you are up to. For tips on Internet safety, check out the BBC's site *http://news.bbc.co.uk/cbbcnews/hi/guides*

Be the Future – First

Twenty years ago no one would have thought you could become a millionaire out of selling tiny pixels on a computer screen like Alex Tew. Millions will be made in the future out of things we can't even imagine yet. Even so, it's worth trying to think about what the next big thing might be.

MILLI-MOUTH

❛The pace of innovation over these next ten years will be much faster than what we have seen in the past.❜
– Microsoft founder Bill Gates

Phones and gadgets are getting more and more clever. Many experts reckon the Internet will be something people can access anywhere, any time, – not just at home, school or work.

This means multi-function gadgets that do everything from allowing you to chat to your mates and book a holiday to watching videos and turning on machines at home. Could you be at the cutting edge of this new technology?

Perhaps you could think of a new idea for sharing information with the expansion in blogs, social networking websites and virtual worlds, like teenage site *www.habbo.com*

Think about how you can now buy music on the net rather than going to a record shop, how people transfer money via computers rather than visiting a bank and even buy cars and houses at the click of a mouse. Could you think of a way that the Internet could be used to help do ordinary things? Are you the future of the techno revolution?

For more info on getting started on the web, try the BBC's special site *www.bbc.co.uk/webwise*

8.
PUT YOUR DREAM
INTO ACTION

**So, it's time for the big questions: what's your goal
and how are you going to make it happen? You've
heard from people in all walks of life about how they
made it to the top and achieved their ambitions. You
have also seen that people who have done brilliantly
didn't usually set out with the dream of making piles
of cash. To make their mark in the world, whether it
was in business, telly, sport, acting or music, they
had to focus on their talents and get the maximum
out of them.**

By now you should be reckoning that becoming a milli-thinker like
them is within your grasp. Although all these millionaires and brilliant
individuals had very different backgrounds, they share many qualities
and there are some great themes in their advice.

The Milli-Magic: The Big Tip-Off

Whether you want to spend your life on the football pitch or in the
boardroom, use these top tips as your guide and a bit of their milli-
magic might just rub off.

On You
★ Believe in yourself and your ideas. Listen to your inner voice.
★ Think about the world around you. What needs changing? What
   can you offer? What inspires you? What is your goal?

★ Do something you enjoy. Try not to see work and life as two different things. Make your hobbies your job.

★ Stay healthy by eating well and doing exercise. This will help the ideas flow.

★ You reap what you sow. Put the effort in. A bit of hard work will pay off.

On the Practical Side

★ Try to do something new – celebrate your difference and make the most of it.

★ Seek help from others – and respect them. Talk and listen to people with experience and think about who else you are going to involve in your dream.

★ Think about money in a different way – how you can save it and make it, not just how to spend it.

★ Get involved, from forming a band to acting in a local play to setting up a business with your mates.

★ Plan your future – be it inventions, music or anything else in which you want to shine. Do your research into it.

Mind Blowing

★ You can start now – no need for millions in the bank or loads of experience.

★ Don't be afraid of failure – it's all part of the process.

★ Enjoy the experience of trying to achieve your goal – as much as making it come true.

★ Remember that money alone doesn't make you happy.

★ Go for it . . . and don't give up.

★ Oh, and good luck!

THANKS
A MILLION . . .

A lot of people gave up their time freely to help us with this book and we'd like to thank all those who gave us interviews: Cecelia Ahern, Trevor Baylis, Oliver Bridge, Tanya Budd, Fraser Doherty, James Dyson, Bryony and Kathryn Frost, Ryan Giggs, Rupert Grint, Isa Guha, Sir Stelios Haji-Ioannou, Alvin Hall, Emma Harrison, Katherine Jenkins, Peter Jones, Amir Khan, Martha Lane Fox, Aaron Lennon, Rupert Loman, Katie Melua, Harry Redknapp, Michael Smith, Sam Stern, Chris Tarrant, Ben Way and Simon Woodroffe. There were also a number of people who gave us their advice and helped make things happen. These include our editor, Jacqui Butler, and our agents, Stephanie Thwaites and Robert Smith. Thanks also to Paul Nero, Steve Gebbett, Alan Kingston, Katie Prescott, Victoria Harris, Samm Taylor, Martin Phillips, Tamsin Moore, Naomi Fruen, Emma Gordon, Stuart Higgins, Fran Bowden, Julia Mitchell, Jenny Wilkinson, Nigel Grint, Natasha Blake, Tom Hadfield, Nick Harris, James Rothnie, Susan Stern, Julia Curry, Vicki McIvor, Sue Harris, Joe O'Neil, Daniel Simister, Leon Angel, Marisa Knightley and Asif Vali.